THE ESSENTIAL GUIDE TO
COMPETITION MATH
(Fundamentals Plus)

유하림(Harim Yoo) 지음

THE ESSENTIAL GUIDE TO
COMPETITION MATH(Fundamentals Plus)

발행 2021년 5월 20일 초판 1쇄
2024년 9월 30일 개정 1쇄

저자 유하림
발행인 최영민
발행처 피앤피북
주소 경기도 파주시 신촌로 16
전화 031-8071-0088
팩스 031-942-8688
전자우편 hermonh@naver.com
출판등록 2015년 3월 27일
등록번호 제406-2015-31호

ⓒ 유하림 2021, Printed in Korea.

ISBN 979-11-94085-13-3 (53410)

- 헤르몬하우스는 피앤피북의 임프린트 출판사입니다.
- 이 책의 어느 부분도 저작권자나 발행인의 승인 없이 무단 복제하여 이용할 수 없습니다.
- 정가는 뒤표지에 있습니다.

❖ 저자직강 인터넷 강의는 SAT, AP No.1 인터넷 강의 사이트인 마스터프랩 (www.masterprep.net) 에서 보실 수 있습니다.

Preface

To. 학부모님과 학생들께

개정판이 나오기까지 이 교재를 구매해주신 학부모님, 그리고 학생 여러분에게 감사의 말씀을 전합니다. The Essential Guide to Competition Math (Fundamentals)는 지금까지 AMC 10/12을 처음 시작하려는 학생들에게 효과적인 교재로, 확인한바, 감사하게도 Teaching Material로도 국내에서 여러 군데서 활용되고 있는 것을 알 수 있었습니다.

2021년 이후, 첫 개정판인 만큼, 기존에 있는 오타 수정을 포함하여, 새로운 주제를 추가하여, 조금 더 많은 문제를 다룰 수 있게 되었습니다. 특히, 리치프렙 학원에서 AMC 1012 입문반 교재로 사용하고 있는 이 교재는 Fundamentals Plus 교재로 개편하게 되면서, 수차례 USAMO Qualifier로 학창 시절을 보낸 매우 똑똑한 학생 임노현 군이 많은 도움을 주었습니다.

The Essential Guide가 암시하듯, 각 주제의 핵심 문제들로 구성되어있습니다. 특히, 책을 구성하고 있는 문제들은 하나하나 미국 경시 수학을 준비하려는 학생들에게 필요한 문제들로 WALK-THROUGH를 통해, 학생들이 혼자서도 풀 수 있는 방식으로 기준을 구성한 책입니다. (Evan Chen에게 Walk-Through 개념을 써도 되겠냐는 허락을 구하였고, 고맙게도 이 용어를 사용해도 된다고 하였습니다.)

이 교재를 출간할 수 있도록 물심양면으로 힘써주신 마스터프랩 권주근 대표님께 감사합니다. 그리고 언제나 든든한 지원군인 제 아내와 딸, 부모님께도 항상 감사합니다. 마지막으로, 제 삶에 이러한 기회를 주신 하나님께 감사드립니다. 앞으로도 더 좋은 교재를 만들어 견고하고 튼튼한 유하림 커리큘럼을 완성하길 희망합니다.

2024년 가을
유하림

이 책의 특징

유하림 커리큘럼 Essential Math Series 경시 시험 대비를 위한 책 중 AMC 10(12), CEMC, ARML Local, Purple Comet Math Meet와 같은 시험을 대비하는 교재입니다. AMC 10을 시작하는 8, 9, 10학년 한국 학생들이 AIME Qualification을 받기 위해 공부해야하는 필독서가 되길 바라는 마음으로 집필하였습니다. 현재 미국 명문 Boarding School 및 국내외 외국인학교에 다니는 8, 9, 10학년 학생들이 AMC 10(12) 및 다른 경시 시험에서 실제로 적극적으로 사고(think)하고, 문제 풀이의 방향을 잡을 수 있길 바라면서 책을 썼습니다.

☝ 입문서로 최적화된 교재

경시 수학 관련하여 압구정 현장 강의에서 많은 학생들을 교육하였고, 실제로 이런 문제들을 포함한 수업을 듣다가, 경시 수학에 연을 맺어, MIT 및 Stanford와 같이 유수의 학교로 간 제자들이 많습니다. 위 제자들을 가르치며, 핵심 개념과 복잡한 문제풀이의 그 중간과정에서 가장 많이 고민했던 유형들의 문제들과 다양한 개념의 융합된 형태의 문제들을 적절히 섞어두었습니다. 위 책은 현장 강의에서 가장 좋은 피드백을 받은 문제들 위주로 작성한 교재이므로, 직접 풀어보고, AMC 10을 시작하는 학생들에게 좋은 입문서입니다.

✌️ 생각의 확장을 위한 교재

단순한 경우의 수부터 시작해서, 여러 생각을 필요로 하는 기하 문제들까지 크게 Counting, Number Theory, Geometry로 구성된 이 책은 쉽고 거침없이 시작할 수 있도록 구성해두었습니다. 실제 AMC에서 나오는 유형보다는 쉽게, 다만 그 문제를 풀기 위해 반드시 알아야하는 방향을 제시하는 교재로 집필하였습니다. 유형으로 나누어 설명하는 것보다, 각 분야별 개념이 어떻게 발전되고, 어떤 식의 사고 방식으로 적용되는지, 그리고 어떻게 합쳐지면서 문제 풀이에 적용되는지 체감하며 공부할 수 있는 교재입니다.

🤟 유학 준비생을 위한 바로 그 교재

교과 수학보다 응용의 폭이 깊어서, 시작조차 엄두를 내지 못했던 유학생들과 그 준비생들에게 하나의 지름길이 될 수 있기를 희망하면서 집필한 책입니다. 노스웨스턴 대학교 학창시절 수학에 대한 열정을 뒤늦게 꽃피워 밤새워 공부했고, 저는 학생들을 더 잘 가르치고, 더 나은 미래로 이끌기 위해, AMC, AIME, ARML, HMMT, PUMaC, SUMO와 같은 문제들을 동일한 열정으로 끊임없이 풀고 해석합니다. 여러분이 지금 보는 이 책은 제 현재 노력의 최선의 산실이며, 앞으로도 그러할 것입니다. 이 책을 통해 수학을 두려워하지 않고, 문제 해결을 즐거워하며, 이른 나이에 수학에 대한 열정을 꽃피우길 기대합니다.

CONTENTS

Preface 3

이 책의 특징 4

Topic 1 Beginning with Combinatorics 9

    1.1   Multiplication and Addition Principle 10

    1.2   Principle of Inclusion and Exclusion 12

    1.3   Practices..13

Topic 2 Continuing with Combinatorics 47

    2.1   Case enumeration and Complements..........................48

    2.2   Indistinguishables and Distinguishables.....................50

            2.2.1 Permutation Allowing Repetitions......................50

            2.2.2 Partition of Sets 50

            2.2.3 Combination Allowing Repetitions.....................51

            2.2.4 Partition of Natural Numbers 51

    2.3   Practices..53

Topic 3 Ending with Combinatorics 83

    3.1   Probability with Restrictions 84

    3.2   More about Probability...86

    3.3   Practices..88

Topic 4 Beginning with Number Theory 127

    4.1   Divisors and Remainders..128

    4.2   Parity and Modular Arithmetic 130

    4.3   Practices..131

Topic 5 Ending with Number Theory 157

    5.1   Divisibility and Modular Arithmetic 158
    5.2   Chinese Remainder Theorem 160
    5.3   Base Expression and Modular Expression 161
    5.4   Practices...162

Topic 6 Beginning with Geometry 191

    6.1   Basic Guidelines for Plane Geometry Problems 192
    6.2   Angle Bisector and Perpendicular Bisector..................195
    6.3   Practices...196

Topic 7 Ending with Geometry 219

    7.1   Quadrilaterals and Cyclic Quadrilaterals......................220
    7.2   Circles 221
    7.3   Practices...222

Topic 8 More About Algebra 2 / Precalculus 245

    8.1   About Polynomials...246
    8.2   Maximum and Minimum..248
    8.3   Floor Function 249
    8.4   Sequence and Series...250
    8.5   Using Trigonometry for Angle Equations....................251
    8.6   Complex Plane Geometry and Vectors.........................252
    8.7   Practices...255

 # List of Math Competitions

Here's a list of some AMC 10/12 or equivalent exams.

1. AMC 10/12A
2. AMC 10/12B
3. AIME (American Invitational Mathematics Examination)
4. USAMO (USA Mathematical Olympiad)
5. HMMT (Harvard-MIT Mathematics Tournament)
6. PUMaC (Princeton University Mathematics Competition)
7. ARML (American Regions Mathematics League)
8. Purple Comet! Math Meet
9. Mandelbrot Competition
10. MathCounts
11. CEMC Exams

Remember to mention that these exams serve as valuable opportunities to test your skills, challenge yourself, and gain valuable experience in math competitions. Participating in these exams will not only help you gauge your progress but also provide exposure to a variety of problem types and competition formats.

Good luck on your math competition journey!

TOPIC 1

Beginning with Combinatorics

1.1 Multiplication and Addition Principle
1.2 Principle of Inclusion and Exclusion
1.3 Practices

1.1 Multiplication and Addition Principle

First off, when do we multiply or add? How do we determine whether we *multiply* or *add* the number of events?

We multiply if

- two events are in a sequence of ongoing action. In fact, they may occur at the same time or in a series of events.

- counts are repetitive. In other words, if prior selection does not interfere with the next action(or selection), we multiply.

Let's have a look at the following example.

Example If there are three menus for breakfast and four menus for lunch, how many combinations of breakfast and lunch menus in total, assuming that one must choose one menu per meal?

Solution Even though we do not eat breakfast and lunch at the same time, we count as if *actions are ongoing*. If you have the feeling of ongoing counting, you keep *multiplying* the number of events. There are 3 menus for breakfast. You have three possibilities to choose one menu. Now, is my count done after choosing one menu for breakfast? No. We must count the number of possible menus for lunch. This is when we *multiply* the number of menus for lunch. Hence, there are 4 menus for lunch. In total, the answer is

$$3 \times 4 = 12$$

How about the feeling of "repetitive counts?" Have a look at the following example.

Example If there are three possible roads from town A to B, and five possible roads from B to C, how many possible routes can you choose to move on from A to C, bypassing B?

Solution This illustrates the feeling of repetitive counts. Regardless of which path you choose from A to B, five roads from B to C are unchanging. In other words, if you choose one path from A to B, there are five paths from B to C that are connected to the path chosen from A to B. Likewise, if you choose different path from A to B, there are still same five paths from B to C. In short, the subsequent counts are repetitive. In this case, we may say future does not change per any path you choose from A to B. In this case, you multiply the number of events.

When do we add? We add if

- we perform caseworks, specifically when the subsequent choice is affected by the prior one.

- two events cannot occur at the same time.

Let's have a look at the following example.

Example If there are three menus for breakfast and four menus for lunch, what is the meaning of $3 + 4$ menus in total, assuming that one must choose at most one menu per meal?

Solution If you choose to eat breakfast only, there are three menus. On the other hand, if you choose to eat lunch, there are only four menus. In other words, if you eat either breakfast or lunch, you add the number of menus.

Caseworks are usually comprehensive and exhaustive. Let's have a look at the following example.

Example If two integers x and y are added, how many possible parities(even/oddness) are there?

Solution First off, x could be either even or odd. Same goes for y. Therefore, there are four cases for the case enumeration.

$(x, y) =$(even,even) $(x, y) =$(even,odd) $(x, y) =$(odd,even) $(x, y) =$(odd,odd)

As you can see from the cases above, enumerating all cases is exhaustive and comprehensive. Any two cases above cannot occur at the same time. Hence, there are four possibilities. However, two events result in equal parities each. Specifically, even+even=odd+odd=even. Likewise, odd+even=even+odd=odd. Therefore, there are two possibilities.

We also add when counts are not repetitive. In fact, future changes as we choose different counts. The following example illustrates this point in detail.

Example Given two digit number $\overline{AB}$, if B is either 0 or 1, find the number of all $\overline{AB}$ such that it is divisible by 3.

Solution If $B = 0$, then $A = 3, 6, 9$ would work. However, if $B = 1$, then $A \neq 3, 6, 9$. The possibilities for A definitely change as we switch from $B = 0$ to $B = 1$. In particular, if $B = 1$, then $A = 2, 5, 8$. Therefore, there are 6 possible values for $\overline{AB}$.

1.2 Principle of Inclusion and Exclusion

This principle, also known as P.I.E, is useful when we get rid of overcounts. First off, we would like to see how 2-set scenario works.

$$n(A \cup B) = n(A) + n(B) - n(A \cap B)$$

While $A \cup B$ is the case where the number of events A or(inclusively) B are counted, $A \cap B$ is the case where the number of events for both A and B are counted. In middle school competitions, we use the following properties.

$$n(A \cup B) + n(A \cap B) = n(A) + n(B)$$

Example Let $U = \{1, 2, 3, \cdots, 100\}$. If A is the set of elements of U that are multiples of 2 and B is the set of elements of U that are multiples of 3, find $n(A \cup B)$.

Solution In order to find $n(A \cup B)$. We compute $n(A)$ first by using floor notation, i.e., $\lfloor \frac{100}{2} \rfloor = 50$ multiples of 2. Similarly, $n(B)$ can be computed as $\lfloor \frac{100}{3} \rfloor = 33$ multiples of 3. How about $n(A \cap B)$? Well, $n(A \cap B)$ can be computed by the number of multiples of 6 that are smaller than or equal to 100, so we compute it as $\lfloor \frac{100}{6} \rfloor = 16$ multiples of 6. Therefore,

$$n(A \cup B) = \lfloor \frac{100}{2} \rfloor + \lfloor \frac{100}{3} \rfloor - \lfloor \frac{100}{6} \rfloor = 50 + 33 - 16 = 67$$

What if we have a 3-set scenario? We could have it added, subtracted for double intersection, and added for triple intersection to find what we need, just as the principle of inclusion-exclusion tells us.

$$n(A \cup B \cup C) = n(A) + n(B) + n(C) - n(A \cap B) - n(A \cap C) - n(B \cap C) + n(A \cap B \cap C)$$

Example If $U = \{1, 2, 3, \cdots, 20\}$, if $A = \{2, 4, 6, \cdots, 20\}$, $B = \{3, 6, 9, \cdots, 18\}$ and $C = \{5, 10, 15, 20\}$, find $n(A \cup B \cup C)$.

Solution

$$\begin{aligned} n(A \cup B \cup C) &= n(A) + n(B) + n(C) - n(A \cap B) - n(A \cap C) - n(B \cap C) + n(A \cap B \cap C) \\ &= 10 + 6 + 4 - 3 - 2 - 1 + 0 \\ &= 14 \end{aligned}$$

where $n(A \cap B)$ refers to the number of multiples of 6 less than or equal to 20, $n(B \cap C)$ refers to the number of multiples of 15 less than or equal to 20, and $n(C \cap A)$ refers to the number of multiples of 10 less than or equal to 20. Lastly, $n(A \cap B \cap C)$ refers to the number of multiples of 30 less than or equal to 20, which does not exist.

1.3 Practices

1. A *palindrome* is a positive integer which reads the same forward and backward such as 2332 or 14541. If there are n number of four-digit palindromes, find the number of positive divisors of n.

Walk-Through

1. Label your four-digit palindromes. For example, a three-digit integer can be expressed as $\overline{abc}$ where $\overline{abc} = 100a + 10b + c$.

2. Find the number of ways to fill up the four-digit palindromes. For each digit, there are 10 possible digits to place in. How about the thousand's digit?

3. Prime factorize n, the number of which is found in step 2. For example, a prime factorization of 12 is $2^2 \cdot 3$.

4. Count the number of divisors by looking at the prime factorization of n. For example, the number of positive divisors of 12 is $(2+1)(1+1) = 3 \cdot 2 = 6$.

2. Suppose there are 24 integers using each of the following digits, 3, 4, 5, and 6 exactly once, and arranged from least to greatest. What is the 15th integer in the arranged order?

Walk-Through

1. Label a four-digit integer first. For example, a three-digit integer may be labeled as $\overline{abc}$ as shown in the previous problem.

2. Fix 3 as the thousands digit. Write the other three digits in letters. Compute the number of permutation of all other three digits when 3 is the thousands digit.

3. Fix 4 as the thousands digit. Write the other three digits in letters. Compute the number of permutation of all other three digits when 4 is the thousands digit.

4. Fix 5 as the thousands digit. Notice that the 15th integer is in this list.

5. Fix 3 as the hundreds digit, assuming that the thousands digit is 5. Label other two digits in letters. Compute the number of permutation of other two digits when 5 is the thousands digit and 3 is the hundreds digit. Hence, compute the 15th integer.

14 The Essential Guide to **Competition Math**(Fundamentals Plus)

3. Given a finite sequence of real numbers $\left\{2\frac{1}{3}, 3, 3\frac{2}{3}, 4\frac{1}{3}, 5, 5\frac{2}{3}, \cdots, 26\frac{1}{3}\right\}$, if the last number is in the nth entry, find n^2.

Walk-Through

1. Let's use one-to-one correspondence. Rewrite the list of real numbers in single-fraction form. (For instance, switch $2\frac{1}{3}$ into $\frac{7}{3}$.)

2. Multiply every term in the list by 3. The number of items in the changed list equals the number of items in the original list.

3. Subtract 1 from every term in the list in step 2.

4. Divide by 2 from every term in the list in step 3.

5. Subtract 2 from every term in the list in step 4. Notice that the number of items in the changed lists is invariant. Find n.

6. Using $(a \pm b)^2 = a^2 \pm 2ab + b^2$, compute n^2.

4. Find the sum of all possible whole numbers that lie in the interval between $\dfrac{\pi}{100}$ and $\dfrac{100}{\pi}$.

> **Walk-Through**
>
> 1. Notice that $\pi \approx 3.14$. Hence, find the smallest whole number greater than $\dfrac{\pi}{100}$ by the Well-Ordering Principle.
>
> 2. Notice that $\dfrac{1}{\pi} \approx 0.318309$. Hence, find the greatest whole number smaller than $\dfrac{100}{\pi}$ by the Well-Ordering Principle.
>
> 3. Let's get the answer by T_n, the nth triangular sum.
>
> 4. Or, use the arithmetic sum formula $S_n = \dfrac{n(a_1 + a_n)}{2}$.

5. Given a sequence of integers, $\{1, 2, 3, \cdots, 9, 100, 101, \cdots, 999, 10000, 10001, \cdots\}$, find the 1000th number in the sequence, which only contains integers with odd number of digits and the numbers are listed from least to greatest.

Walk-Through

1. Compute the number of single-digit numbers.

2. Label 100 as the 10th number in the sequence. Then, 101 is the 11th term in the sequence. Then, compute the position of 999 in the sequence using one-to-one correspondence.

3. Next to 999, there is 10000. If 100 is the Nth term in the sequence, notice that 10000 is the $(N+1)$th term.

4. Now, reverse-engineer to find out 1000th term in the sequence.

6. Suppose there is a sequence of positive single digits that are alternately counting up and down, i.e.,

$$\{1, 2, 3, 4, 5, 6, 7, 8, 9, 8, 7, 6, 5, 4, 3, 2, 1, 2, 3, 4, \cdots\}$$

Find the 123456th integer in the sequence above.

Walk-Through

1. Notice that the terms are repetitive. Determine the size of a bundle that keeps repeating.

2. Divide 123456 by the size of the bundle.

3. Interpret the meaning of the quotient and the remainder.

4. Find the 123456th term by using the remainder found in step 3.

7. Every year divisible by 4 is called a leap year, except for years which are divisible by 100. On the other hand, some years that are multiples of 100 are leap years, i.e., years divisible by 400. How many *leap years* are there between 2001 and 2999?

Walk-Through

1. Label "a multiple of 4" into a mathematical expression. (For instance, even integer can be written as $2k$ for some integer k, whereas odd integer can be written as $2k+1$ for some integer k.)

2. Make sure that the expression found in step 1 is between 2001 and 2009. Hence, count the number of multiples of 4 between 2001 and 2999.

3. Label "a multiple of 100" into a mathematical expression, like the one in step 1. Put the expression between 2001 and 2999. Hence, count the number of multiples of 100 between 2001 and 2999.

4. Label "a multiple of 400" into a mathematical expression. Repeat the process in step 3.

5. Now, count the number of leap years between 2001 and 2999.

8. Suppose there are six non-negative integers, not necessarily distinct, $\{8, a, b, 9, 12, 13\}$ and its mean value (arithmetic average) is 10. Find the number of all possible ordered pairs (a, b).

> **Walk-Through**
>
> 1. Set the average equation using a and b.
>
> 2. Directly count the number of ordered pairs (a, b) by solving the equation found in step 1.
>
> 3. Or, try find a pair (a, b) that makes sense for the equation found in step 1. In particular, find it by setting $b = 0$.
>
> 4. Keep subtracting 1 to a, while adding 1 to b. See what happens to the summation. Continue doing it until $a = 0$. Compare the result found in step 2.
>
> 5. (Additional) In order to practice Diophantine equation, solve $20x + 23y = 2023$ for non-negative integers x and y. Make sure you find all 5 pairs.

9. If both positive integers, $3n$ and $\dfrac{n}{3}$, have four digits, compute the number of possible integer values of n.

Walk-Through

1. Write the inequality for $3n$. For example, if x is between 1 and 10, we write $1 < x < 10$. Hence, compute the number of n satisfying the inequality.

2. Write the inequality for $\dfrac{n}{3}$. Hence, compute the number of n satisfying the inequality.

3. Find the set of common integers for step 1 and step 2.

4. Look closely at the condition that $\dfrac{n}{3}$ is positive integer. Now, solve the problem according to the condition found in step 4.

10. In a group of 30 students, 8 take Combinatorics, 12 take Number Theory and 3 take both subjects. How many students of the group take neither Combinatorics nor Number Theory?

> **Walk-Through**
>
> 1. Label C and N as the set of students taking Combinatorics and Number Theory, respectively. Rewrite the given information in expressions.
>
> 2. De Morgan's Law states that $A^c \cap B^c = (A \cup B)^c$ where A^c stands for the complement of A. Compute $|A \cup B|$.
>
> 3. Compute the number of students not in $A \cup B$.

11. At Math School, all students study at least one out of three subjects: Geometry, Combinatorics and Number Theory. 3 students take all three subjects, 21 students do two or more subjects, half of all students participate in Combinatorics, and the ratio of students taking Geometry, Combinatorics, and Number Theory, respectively, is $3:4:5$. Find the total number of students in Math School.

> **Walk-Through**
>
> 1. Label the set of students taking Geometry, Combinatorics, and Number Theory as G, C and N, respectively.
>
> 2. Paraphrase $G:C:N = 3:4:5$ into $G = 3k$, $C = 4k$ and $N = 5k$ for some whole number k.
>
> 3. Find the total number of students in terms of k.
>
> 4. Write an expression for 21 students taking two or more subjects.
>
> 5. Use the principle of inclusion and exclusion to solve for k.

12. There are 360 people in Payoff school. 15 take Geometry, English, and Literature, and 15 don't take any of them. 180 take Geometry. Twice as many students take Literature as they take English. 75 take both Geometry and Literature, and 75 take both English and Literature. Only 30 take both English and Geometry. How many students take English?

> **Walk-Through**
>
> 1. Label the set of students taking Geometry, English, and Literature.
>
> 2. Paraphrase all statements in terms of set notations.
>
> 3. Let n be the number of students taking English. Write an equation for "Twice as many students take Literature as they take English."
>
> 4. Use the principle of inclusion and exclusion to solve for n.

13. Out of all integers n such that $1 \leq n \leq 2005$, how many integers are multiples of 3 or 4 but not 12?

Walk-Through

1. Label "multiples of 3" and count the number of multiples of 3 in the given inequality.

2. Or, compute $\left\lfloor \dfrac{2005}{3} \right\rfloor$. Compare this with the answer found in step 1.

3. Label "multiples of 4" and count the number of multiples of 4 in the given inequality.

4. Or, compute $\left\lfloor \dfrac{2005}{4} \right\rfloor$. Compare this with the answer found in step 3.

5. Label "multiples of 12" and count the number of multiples of 12 in the given inequality. Like step 2 and 4, use floor function to find the number of multiples of 12.

6. Read the part "multiples of 3 and 4, but not 12" carefully. One must take out the common part twice.

14. How many odd five-digit positive integers can be formed by choosing digits from the set $\{3, 4, 5, 6, 7\}$ while digits can be repeated?

Walk-Through

1. Construct $\overline{abcde}$ for digits a, b, c, d, and e.

2. Look for binding condition, i.e., the last digit being odd.

3. Find the set of common integers for step 1 and step 2.

4. Look closely at the condition that $\frac{n}{3}$ is positive integer. Now, solve the problem according to the condition found in step 4.

15. If there are n number of 5-digit positive integers such that it contains at least one digit repeated, find the value of $\left\lfloor \dfrac{n}{9} \right\rfloor$.

Walk-Through

1. Count the total number of five-digit positive integers by labeling a 5-digit integer as $\overline{abcde}$.

2. Consider a case when no digit is repeated. Count the number of cases when no digit is repeated for a 5-digit integer. This is called "complementary counting."

3. Subtract a number found in step 2 from a number found in step 1.

4. Compute $\left\lfloor \dfrac{n}{9} \right\rfloor$.

5. For side notes, if $\dfrac{a}{b}$ is an integer N, then $\left\lfloor \dfrac{a}{b} \right\rfloor$ is the same integer because rounding down an integer does not change the result. Otherwise, for $N < \dfrac{a}{b} < N+1$, it is conveniently known that $\left\lfloor \dfrac{a}{b} \right\rfloor = N$.

16. Let p be the number of 3-letter "words" that can be formed from all possible alphabets, where the first letter is a vowel, and q be the number of 3-letter "words" that can be formed from the same set of alphabets, where the first letter is a vowel and all three letters are distinct. If p/q is reduced to the lowest term so that $p/q = m/n$ where m and n are relatively prime, find the sum of m and n.

Walk-Through

1. Notice that vowels are $\{a, e, i, o, u\}$. Construct a three-letter word as ABC.

2. In order to count p, we must use the set of all alphabets, which consists of 26 alphabets. Notice that the first letter must be selected out of vowels, and this three-letter word allows repeated letters.

3. On the other hand, in order to count q, use the condition that no letter is repeated. In order to compute the cases when letter is not repeated, try with specific cases.

4. Let the first letter be a vowel, let's say a. Then, compute how many letters are left in the set of alphabets for the second letter in a three-letter word.

5. Let the second letter be b. Then, compute how many letters are left in the set of alphabets for the third letter in a three-letter word.

6. Finish computing q, and compare p and q to finish solving the problem.

17. If there are n four-letter words that start and end with the same alphabet, the sum of all positive divisors of n can be written as

$$\sum_{k=0}^{r} p^k \times \sum_{k=0}^{r} q^k$$

Find the difference between n and $(pq)^r$.

> **Walk-Through**
>
> 1. Construct a four-letter word as $\overline{x_1 x_2 x_3 x_4}$, where $x_1 = x_4$.
>
> 2. Recall that there are 26 alphabets to fill x_1, x_2, and x_3, respectively.
>
> 3. Given $n = (pq)^r$ for some prime p and q, the sum of divisors of n equals $(1 + p + p^2 + \cdots + p^r)(1 + q + q^2 + \cdots + q^r)$. For instance, if $n = 36 = 2^2 3^2$, it is easy to check that the sum of divisors is $(1 + 2 + 2^2)(1 + 3 + 3^2)$.
>
> 4. Use step 3 to find the the difference between n and pq^r.

TOPIC 1 Beginning with Combinatorics

18. Suppose there are five cards with letters A, B, C, D, and E, and four cards with numbers 1, 2, 3, and 4. If all nine cards are rearranged, there are n arrangements such that B is adjacent to two cards with numbers on its right and left, find the number of odd divisors of n.

> **Walk-Through**
>
> 1. Construct nine spots to begin with, i.e., ☐☐☐☐☐☐☐☐☐.
>
> 2. Let $(\star, B, \star)$ be a triple such that B is adjacent to two cards with numbers on its right and left.
>
> 3. Notice that B cannot be placed in the first box or last box. Find out the number of places where B can be placed.
>
> 4. Then, find out the number of ways to fill the two stars with numbers.
>
> 5. Lastly, find out the number of ways to fill the other boxes with remaining letters and numbers.
>
> 6. Multiply the number of cases found in step 3, 4, and 5, altogether.

19. How many ways are there to divide a group of 6 mathletes among Math Club, Math Circle, and Math Team, all of which are different club activities? (Each team could have anywhere from 0 to 6 of mathletes on it. Assume the friends are distinguishable.)

> **Walk-Through**
>
> 1. Notice that mathletes are all different. Also, the clubs are all distinguishable. This must be permutation allowing repetition.
>
> 2. Find out the number of ways that the first mathlete chooses his or her club.
>
> 3. Find out the number of ways that the second mathlete chooses his or her club. Continue to do so for other mathletes.
>
> 4. Notice that there may be a club without any member.
>
> 5. Multiply the number of ways found in step 2 and step 3 altogether.

20. Consider the rectangular region whose vertices are $(10, 3)$, $(0, 3)$, $(0, -5)$, $(10, -5)$. How many lattice points are located in the interior of the rectangle? (Lattice points are points with integer coordinates.)

> **Walk-Through**
>
> 1. Label a lattice point as (x, y). Here, a lattice point is a point with integer coordinates.
>
> 2. Set up an inequality that satisfies the given condition for x.
>
> 3. Set up an inequality that satisfies the given condition for y.
>
> 4. Find the number of x's and y's satisfying the step 2 and 3.
>
> 5. Multiply the numbers found in step 4 and conclude the problem.

21. Subway offers its sandwiches with the following condiments: ketchup, sweet onion sauce, marinara sauce, tomato, lettuce, olives, Parmesan cheese, and jalapenos. A customer can choose either one, two, or three meatballs, and any collection of condiments. If there are n different kinds of sandwiches that can be ordered, and the sum of its positive divisors has 4-digit numbers, find its last two digits.

> **Walk-Through**
>
> 1. Underline "any collection of condiments." Paraphrase it
>
> 2. One may choose to put ketchup or not. Likewise, one may choose to put sweet onion sauce or not. Continue this process for all condiments.
>
> 3. Find the number of ways to choose meatball(s).
>
> 4. Multiply number of cases found in step 2 and 3.
>
> 5. Call a number found in step 4 as n.
>
> 6. Prime factorize n and find the sum of divisors and conclude solving the problem.

22. Alice, Bob, and Charlie want to buy one book each at a bookstore where there are 15 non-fictions, 6 comic books and 8 fantasy novels. They each wish different types. How many ways can Alice, Bob, and Charlie buy books and be satisfied?

> **Walk-Through**
>
> 1. Choose types of books for Alice, Bob, and Charlie.
>
> 2. Assume that Alice chooses a non-fiction, Bob a comic book, and Charlie a fantasy novel.
>
> 3. Count the number of cases Alice chooses one book out of 15 books.
>
> 4. Count the number of cases Bob chooses a book out of 6 comic books.
>
> 5. Count the number of cases Charlie chooses a book out of 8 fantasy novels.
>
> 6. Multiply the number of cases found in step 1, 3, 4, and 5, by the principle of multiplication.

23. A cuisine restaurant offers three types of appetizers, and exactly twice as many desserts as main courses. The most popular dinner course consists of an appetizer, a main course, and a dessert. What is the least number of main courses that the restaurant should offer for this popular dinner course so that a customer could have a different dinner every night in the year 2021?

Walk-Through

1. Let n be the number of main courses. Compute the number of desserts.

2. Choose 1 main course, 1 dessert, and 1 appetizer.

3. Notice that there are 365 days in year 2021. Set up an inequality with the number of dinner courses found in step 2.

4. By trial and error, find the smallest possible n values satisfying the inequality in step 3.

24. Let p be the number of 3-digit positive integers that do not contain any of the digits 2, 3, 4 or 5, and q be the number of 3-digit positive integers that do not contain any of the digits 2, 3, 4, or 5, and have no repeated digits. If p/q is reduced to the lowest term so that $p/q = m/n$ where m and n are relatively prime, find the sum of m and n.

> **Walk-Through**
>
> 1. In order to compute p, construct a three digit integer $\overline{abc}$, where each digit cannot be either 2, 3, 4, or 5.
>
> 2. On the other hand, in order to compute q, all digits must be different.
>
> 3. There are two possible ways of computing q : direct counting or complementary counting.
>
> 4. In order to directly count, choose any valid digit for a, and start counting the number of valid digits for b and c, respectively.
>
> 5. In order to count complements, assume all digits are equal, or some digits are equal. Count the number of integers in each case. Now, take these cases out of total cases, and check that the number found in step 3 and 4 are equal.
>
> 6. Simplify $\dfrac{p}{q}$ to solve the problem.

25. If there are n distinct IDs that consist of 2 letters followed by 2 digits, such that one of the digits is odd and the other is even, find the value of $\left\lfloor \dfrac{n}{100} \right\rfloor$.

> **Walk-Through**
>
> 1. Construct four spots for an ID in the problem.
>
> 2. The first two spots must be filled with alphabets. Notice there is no restriction for alphabets. Compute the number of ways to fill these two spots with 26 alphabets each.
>
> 3. The second two spots can be either (even,odd) or (odd,even). Compute the number of cases for each possibility.
>
> 4. Multiply by the numbers found in step 2 and 3.

TOPIC 1 Beginning with Combinatorics

26. 2021 circles are all in the same size. Each pair of these circles overlap but no circle is exactly on top of another circle. Let n be the greatest possible number of total intersection points of these 2021 circles. Compute the value of $n - 2020^2$.

Walk-Through

1. Count the number of intersection between any pair of two circles.

2. Count the number of pair of two circles that can be formed out of 2021 circles.

3. The condition for maximal number of intersection points assume that all points of intersection are distinct.

4. Hence, multiply the number found in step 1 and step 2.

5. When computing $n-2020^2$, use algebraic manipulation for faster computation.

27. The following figure only shows a 6 by 3 dimension mold with six L-shaped figures that consist of three unit squares perfectly fitting the mold. If the larger figure has a 20 by 3 dimension with more L-shaped figures fitting the mold, how many different shapes in total are there to fit a 20 × 3 figure?

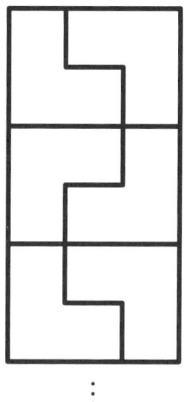

⋮

> **Walk-Through**
>
> 1. Count the number of ways of filling a 2×3 mold by two L-shaped figures.
>
> 2. Count the number of 2×3 molds in a 20×3 figure.
>
> 3. Each of 2×3 mold has to be filled up in a number of ways found in step 1.
>
> 4. Notice that this is an application of permutation allowing repetition.

TOPIC 1 Beginning with Combinatorics

28. A group of 10 Northwestern students go to Norris Center for lunch. Each student eats at either Chipotle or Asian Cuisine. In how many different ways can the students collectively go to lunch?

> **Walk-Through**
>
> 1. The first student can go to either Chipotle or Asian Cuisine.
>
> 2. The second student can go to either Chipotle or Asian Cuisine, as well.
>
> 3. Continue this process until the tenth student chooses the restaurant.
>
> 4. Multiply the number of cases found in step 1, 2, and 3, altogether, by the principle of multiplication.

29. In how many ways can 8 students be seated around a square table with 2 people on each side? If one configuration is rotated to equal other configuration, the two are considered equal.

> **Walk-Through**
>
> 1. There are two ways of solving this problem - either constructive count or getting rid of overcounts. Let's start with constructive count.
>
> 2. How many seats would the first student distinguish?
>
> 3. Make sure the first student be seated. Then, the remaining students will sit down relative to the first student.
>
> 4. Multiply the numbers found in step 2 and 3.
>
> 5. Now, for getting rid of overcount, let all students be seated 8 seats fixed, not allowed to be rotated.
>
> 6. Count the number of lines of symmetry.
>
> 7. Divide the number found in step 5 by a number found in step 6. Compare this number with the answer found in step 4. They are equal.

30. Bob, a math professor at MIT, is assigning grades to a class of 10 bright students at Topology, where he only gives out A^+s, A_0s, and A^-s. The professor can assign grades to all his students in p^q number of ways such that p is a prime number. Find $p + q$.

> **Walk-Through**
>
> 1. The first student may receive one of the three grades.
>
> 2. Likewise, the second student may receive one of the three grades.
>
> 3. Continue this process until the last student receives his grade.
>
> 4. Multiply the numbers found in step 1, 2, and 3, by the principle of multiplication.

Answer Key

1. 12

Let it be written as $ABBA$. Then, there are 9 choices for A and 10 choices for B. Hence, we get $9 \times 10 \times 1 \times 1 = 90$. The prime factorization of this number equals $2^1 3^2 5^1$. Hence, the number of positive divisors must be $2 \times 3 \times 2 = 12$.

2. 5436

Let it begin with $3\square\square\square$. There are $3! = 6$ possibilities. Likewise, $4\square\square\square$ has $3! = 6$ possibilities. Now, $53\square\square$ has two possibilities. Therefore, the 15th number must be 5436.

3. 1369

It starts from $7/3$ and ends at $79/3$, multiply the set of numbers by 3 and add 1 and divide by 2 and subtract 3, all of which preserves one-to-one correspondence. Hence, we get the final list of $\{1, 2, 3, \cdots, 37\}$. There are 37 numbers in total. Therefore, $37^2 = 1369$ is the answer.

4. 496

$\frac{\pi}{100}$ is less than 1 and $\frac{100}{\pi} = 31.83$.
Hence, there are 31 integers starting from 1. The sum of this number must be $\frac{31(1+31)}{2} = 496$.

5. 10090

There are 9 single-digit numbers and 900 numbers between 100 and 999, inclusive. Hence, 10000 becomes the 910th number. Using the one-to-one correspondence, we get 10090 as the 1000th number.

6. 2

The sequence reiterates in the cycle of 16 numbers. Divide 123456 by 16 to get the remainder of 0. Hence, the last number of the one whole bundle must be the answer, i.e., 2.

7. 242

$\lfloor \frac{999}{4} \rfloor - \lfloor \frac{999}{100} \rfloor + \lfloor \frac{999}{400} \rfloor = 242$

8. 19

Since the sum of all numbers must be equal to 60, we get $a + b = 18$. Listing all possibilities, we get
$(a, b) = (18, 0), \cdots, (0, 18)$. There are 19 pairs in total.

9. 112

Since $1000 \leq 3n \leq 9999$ and $1000 \leq \frac{n}{3} \leq 9999$, we get $3000 \leq n \leq 3333$.
Since $\frac{n}{3}$ is a whole number, compute the number of multiples of 3. Hence, there are 112 multiples of 3.

10. 13

Using the principle of inclusion and exclusion, we get

$n(C) + n(N) - n(C \cap N) = 8 + 12 - 3 = 17$

Hence, the number of students who take neither Combinatorics nor Number Theory must be $30 - 17 = 13$.

11. 48

First, $n(G \cap C \cap N) = 3$. Second, $n(G \cap C) + n(C \cap N) + n(N \cap G) - 2(3) = 21$, so we get

$$n(G \cap C) + n(C \cap N) + n(N \cap G) = 27$$

Let T be the total number of students at Math School. The principle of inclusion and exclusion implies that

$$\frac{3T}{8} + \frac{T}{2} + \frac{5T}{8} - 27 + 3 = T$$

Hence, $T = 48$. (You can also write $G = 3k$, $C = 4k$, $N = 5k$, so $U = 8k$ to solve a linear equation.)

12. 110

Let the number of students who take English as x. Then, that for Literature must be $2x$. By the principle of inclusion and exclusion, we get $x + 2x + 180 - 75 - 75 - 30 + 15 = 345$. It is not 360 because there are some students not taking any of the class. Hence, $x = 110$.

13. 835

$\lfloor \frac{2005}{3} \rfloor + \lfloor \frac{2005}{4} \rfloor - \lfloor \frac{2005}{12} \rfloor - \lfloor \frac{2005}{12} \rfloor = 835$, eliminating intersections.

14. 1875

There are three possibilities for the last digit, and five possibilities for each other digit. Hence, $3 \times 5^4 = 1875$ is the answer.

15. 6976

Since $n = 9 \times 10^4 - 9(9 \cdot 8 \cdot 7 \cdot 6) = 9 \times 6976$, we get $\lfloor \frac{n}{9} \rfloor = 6976$.

16. 319

Since $p = 5 \times 26 \times 26$ and $q = 5 \times 25 \times 24$, it is reduced to $\frac{m}{n} = \frac{169}{150}$, and the answer is 319.

17. 0

First, $n = 26^3$. Hence, $n = 2^3 \cdot 13^3$. The number of positive divisors of n can be written as

$$(1 + 2 + 2^2 + 2^3)(1 + 13 + 13^2 + 13^3)$$

Hence, $(pq)^r = 26^3$. The difference between n and $(pq)^r$ is 0.

18. 16

Consider $(\square B \square)\square\square \cdots \square$. There are 12 different ways to fill the parentheses and 7! possible ways to configure all these numbers, considering the parentheses as one bundle. If you consider a bundle as a whole number, then there are seven spots to fill up. Hence, we get $7! \times 12$. Its prime factorization turns out to be $2^6 \cdot 3^3 \cdot 5^1 \cdot 7^1$. The number of odd divisors must be $4 \times 2 \times 2 = 16$.

19. 729

For each mathlete, there are three possible clubs to choose. Hence, there are 3^6 possible ways for them to join clubs.

20. 63

There are 7 x-values and 9 y-values to choose. Hence, you simply multiply these two numbers to get all possible lattice points.

21. 44

There are three ways to choose the number of meatballs and 2^8 ways to choose any condiment. Hence, n must be 3×2^8. The sum of its positive divisors must be
$(1+3)(1+2+2^2+\cdots+2^8) = 2044$. Hence, the last two digits must be 44.

22. 4320

Let Alice, Bob and Charlie choose whichever pet type they want. Then, after they choose their favorite types, choose a pet out of the pool we have, i.e.,

$$(3 \times 2 \times 1) \times 15 \times 6 \times 8 = 4320$$

As one can see, the first parentheses computes the number of ways for these three people to choose their types of pets, and the next three numbers give the number of pets for respective kinds.

23. 8

Let n be the number of main courses. Then, there are $2n$ number of desserts. Hence, $3 \times n \times 2n \geq 365$. The smallest possible value of whole number n is 8.

24. 14

First, $p = 5 \times 6 \times 6$. Second, $q = 5 \times 5 \times 4$. Hence, $\frac{p}{q}$ can be reduced to $\frac{9}{5}$. Thus, the answer is 14.

25. 338

Since $n = 26 \times 26 \times 5 \times 5 \times 2$, we get

$$\lfloor \frac{n}{100} \rfloor = 338$$

26. 2020

The number of intersection points between 2021 circles must be $\binom{2021}{2} \times 2$. Hence, $n = 2021 \times 2020$. Therefore, $2021 \times 2020 - 2020^2 = 2020$. Think about making "links" between any two circles, none of which are overlapping. Let a_n be the number of intersection points between n circles. Then, we produce layers of intersection points by $a_n = n(n-1) = n^2 - n$.

27. 1024

There are 2 possible layouts for each rectangle stacked up in 10 stories. Hence, 2^{10} number of configurations can be produced in this set up.

28. 1024

Each student may choose either Chipotle or Asian Cuisine, which is binomial expansion. There are 2 possibilities per student. Since there are 10 number of students, we get 2^{10} possibilities.

29. 10080

Let the first student choose his spot. There are only two distinguishable seats for the first student. As soon as he seats, all the other seats are distinguishable (by the first student), so we get $2 \times 7!$.

30. 13

A typical extension of binomial expansion. Since each student may get one of the three grades, while there are 10 bright students in Bob's class, we get $3^{10} = p^q$. Hence, $p + q = 3 + 10 = 13$.

TOPIC 1 Beginning with Combinatorics

 # Guidance for Studying Competition Math

Studying for competition math can often be an intimidating journey, leaving many feeling uncertain about where to begin or how to proceed. This uncertainty can stem from the complexity of the material, the vast array of topics covered, and the pressure to perform well in competitive settings. It's entirely normal to experience doubts and questions along the way.

However, amidst this uncertainty, one thing remains steadfast: the power of consistency and persistence. While there may not be a straightforward or easy route to mastering competition math, committing to a consistent study routine and persistently tackling challenging problems can yield significant results over time.

Consistency in study habits, such as setting aside dedicated time each day or week to engage with math concepts, builds a strong foundation of understanding and familiarity with the material. This regular practice not only reinforces key concepts but also helps to develop problem-solving skills and strategies essential for success in competitions.

Moreover, persistence plays a crucial role in overcoming obstacles and pushing through moments of difficulty or frustration. It's natural to encounter problems that seem insurmountable or concepts that feel elusive, but persistently working through these challenges, seeking help when needed, and not giving up in the face of setbacks can lead to breakthroughs and deeper understanding.

By emphasizing the importance of consistency and persistence, aspiring mathematicians can find reassurance and support in knowing that progress is achievable through dedicated effort and determination. Each step taken, no matter how small, brings them closer to their goals and eventual success in competition math.

TOPIC 2

Continuing with Combinatorics

2.1 Case enumeration and Complements
2.2 Indistinguishables and Distinguishables
2.3 Practices

2.1 Case enumeration and Complements

The skill set for case enumeration is prerequisite for competition math. That being said, casework could be performed in many different forms, so we have to remember one rule.

Try case-working until it fails.

Types of questions we see for caseworking may appear in the form of integer questions or real number questions. Let's have a look at the following example.

Example Given $m + n = 5$, where m, n are non-negative integers, find all pairs of (m, n).

Solution A typical case-working question since you have two integer variables with the invariant sum. We try out with the following cases.

$$\begin{aligned} m + n &= 5 + 0 \\ &= 4 + 1 \\ &= 3 + 2 \\ &= 2 + 3 \\ &= 1 + 4 \\ &= 0 + 5 \\ &= -1 + 6 \end{aligned}$$

Alright, we stop the process here. As you see the last step. $-1 + 6$ is not the sum of two non-negative integers. Hence, you should eliminate the last step and leave the answer with (m, n) as $(5, 0), (4, 1), (3, 2), (2, 3), (1, 4)$ and $(0, 5)$.

How about the case-working for real numbers? Although this may not be covered in this book, I would like to say that real numbers are extremely useful because they have magnitudes to compare. In other words, if you throw me two real numbers x and y, I have three possible cases to cover : $x < y$, $x = y$ and $x > y$. Let's have a look at the following example.

Example If 1, x, and y are three sides of the triangle where $0 < x < 1$ and $0 < y < 1$, how many different cases of side triples do we have?

Solution Since they are all real numbers, you can always compare the three numbers. First off, $x < 1$ and $y < 1$. So, we have the upper-bound of 1 for both x and y. On the other hand, given $x, y \in \mathbb{R}$, we may have three possible cases.

$$x < y < 1 \qquad\qquad x = y < 1 \qquad\qquad y < x < 1$$

The next skillset we would like to delve into is complementary counting. When do we use complements? We use the skill set when

- there are too many cases in the actual set-up of the question, containing the phrases such as "at least" or "at most."
- there are symmetrical forms in the total counts.

The first bullet-point is quite obvious, but the second one is not. Let's have a look at two examples in detail to see what these gut-feelings are.

Example How many 3-digit positive integers have at least one digit that is a 1 or a 2?

Solution As one can see, the caseworking for at least a 1 or a 2 might be challenging (yet doable). You may have to consider the case where there is only one 1 without 2, two 1s without 2, one 1 with one 2 or two 2s, and so on. The other way around to tackle this question is to highlight "at least." If we count all 3-digit numbers without any 1 or 2, we may have the counts that we should eliminate. The total number of 3-digit positive integers are $9 \times 10 \times 10$, while 3-digit numbers without using 1 or 2 can be counted as $7 \times 8 \times 8$. Hence, the answer we want is $900 - 448 = 452$.

Then, what is the second bullet-point? What does it mean to have a symmetrical form in total counts? The following example illustrates this point directly.

Example If you flip a fair coin 10 times, what is the total number of counts when there are more heads than tails?

Solution First off, having more heads than tails is equivalent to having more tails than heads. As you can see, the probability of getting a head is exactly same as that of getting a tail. In other words, if we eliminate the number of counts when there are equal heads and tails, we get double the amount of counts when there are more heads than tails. The total number of counts is 2^{10}, whereas the number of counts when there are equal number of heads and tails is $\frac{10!}{5!5!}$, i.e., the arrangement of $HHHHHTTTTT$ in a straight line, so this must be combination with repeated letters.[1] Therefore, the answer must be

$$\frac{2^{10} - \frac{10!}{5!5!}}{2}$$

---

[1]Think about $APPLE$. When we arrange $APPLE$ in a straight line, we start with AP_1P_2LE. Then, it must be 5! to arrange the five letters. However, since the original letters have no subscripts, $\square P_1 \square \square P_2$ and $\square P_2 \square \square P_1$ are in fact equivalent. This indicates that there are overcounts. Hence, you divide 5! by 2!, which is the number of arrangements between P_1 and P_2. Hence, the answer is $5!/2!$.

2.2 Indistinguishables and Distinguishables

There are four ways to remember indistinguishables and distinguishables. First, we must understand the basic set-up of a question. It shall always be distributing certain marbles to the plates. However, the shapes of marbles and plates can be categorized into four cases.

- Distinct marbles into distinct plates : permutation allowing repetition

- Distinct marbles into identical-looking plates : partition of sets

- Identical-looking marbles into distinct plates : combination allowing repetition

- Identical-looking marbles into identical-looking plates : partition of natural numbers

2.2.1 Permutation Allowing Repetition

Definition: A permutation allowing repetition refers to the number of ways to arrange n items into k positions where each item can be chosen more than once.

Formula:
$$k^n$$

where k is the number of available choices for each position, and n is the number of positions to fill.

Example: Choosing one of three letters (A, B, C) for each of five positions yields $3^5 = 243$ permutations.

2.2.2 Partition of Sets

Definition: A partition of a set is a way of dividing the set into non-empty subsets such that each element of the original set is included in exactly one subset.

Notation: For a set S, a partition P is a collection $\{P_1, P_2, \ldots, P_k\}$ where:

- $P_i \neq \emptyset$ for all i.

- $P_i \cap P_j = \emptyset$ for all $i \neq j$.

- $\bigcup_{i=1}^{k} P_i = S$.

Example: The set $\{1, 2, 3\}$ can be partitioned as $\{\{1\}, \{2, 3\}\}$, $\{\{1, 2\}, \{3\}\}$, $\{\{1\}, \{2\}, \{3\}\}$, or $\{\{1, 2, 3,\}\}$.

2.2.3 Combination Allowing Repetitions

Definition: A combination allowing repetition (also known as combinations with replacement) refers to the number of ways to choose k elements from n available elements where each element can be chosen more than once, and the order of selection does not matter.

Formula:
$$\binom{n+k-1}{k}$$

where $\binom{n+k-1}{k}$ is the binomial coefficient, representing the number of ways to choose k elements from n types with repetition allowed.

Example: Choosing 3 candies from 5 types (where order does not matter) can be done in $\binom{5+3-1}{3} = \binom{7}{3} = 35$ ways.

2.2.4 Partition of Natural Numbers

Definition: A partition of a natural number n is a way of writing n as a sum of positive integers, where the order of the summands does not matter.

Notation: A partition of n is represented as $n = a_1 + a_2 + \cdots + a_k$, where a_i are positive(or oftentimes, non-negative) integers and $a_1 \geq a_2 \geq \cdots \geq a_k \geq 0$.

Example: The number 3 can be partitioned as 3, $2+1$, or $1+1+1$.

As a recap, let's go over all four cases in the following examples.

Example How many ways can 5 people choose one letter from A, B, and C? (Assume that there could be letters that are not selected by anyone.)

Solution The first person has 3 possible options. The second one has 3 possible options, as well. Since there are 5 people, all of whom are distinct, we get 3^5. This type of counting is called "permutation allowing repetition."

Example How many ways are there to group 5 people in three groups? (Assume that there could be letters that are not selected by anyone.)

Solution We put different marbles into identical-looking plates. We first look at the partition of natural numbers

$$5 = 5 + 0 + 0$$
$$= 4 + 1 + 0$$
$$= 3 + 2 + 0$$
$$= 3 + 1 + 1$$
$$= 2 + 2 + 1$$

There are five possible cases to partition 5 into three groups. Then, we use the partition of sets. Hence, we get $\binom{5}{5}$, $\binom{5}{4}\binom{1}{1}$, $\binom{5}{3}\binom{2}{2}$, $\binom{5}{3}\binom{2}{1}\binom{1}{1}\frac{1}{2!}$, and $\binom{5}{2}\binom{3}{2}\binom{1}{1}\frac{1}{2!}$. The reason why we divide by 2! is that some of the cases have overcounts. For example, suppose there are $\{A, B, C, D, E\}$. If we divide this into $\{A, B, C\}, \{D\}, \{E\}$, we may overcount this by considering it different from $\{A, B, C\}, \{E\}, \{D\}$. In fact, they are exactly equal partitions. This is the reason why we divide some of the counts by 2!.

Example If $a + b + c = 5$, where a, b, and c are nonnegative integers, how many triples (a, b, c) are there?

Solution We place identical-looking marbles into different plates. This is a typical application of combination allowing repetitions. It uses circles and bars. Imagine there are 5 identical-looking circles and two bars. Suppose we are given with $(a, b, c) = (5, 0, 0)$. We would like to have a 1–to–1 correspondence with ○○○○○||. How about $(a, b, c) = (3, 1, 1)$? We get ○○○|○|○. The total number of triples (a, b, c) is $\frac{7!}{2!5!}$.

Example Partition 5 into three nonnegative integers.

Solution The way to take a partition of natural numbers is to use the following strategy. Let $x \geq y \geq z$. Then, we would like to see all possible combinations of (x, y, z) satisfying $x + y + z = 5$. Hence,

$$5 = 5 + 0 + 0$$
$$= 4 + 1 + 0$$
$$= 3 + 2 + 0$$
$$= 3 + 1 + 1$$
$$= 2 + 2 + 1$$

2.3 Practices

1. If $\overline{abc}$ is a 3-digit number such that $b = \dfrac{a+c}{2}$, how many such $\overline{abc}$'s exist, assuming that a, b, and c are not necessarily distinct?

Walk-Through

1. This problem is a classic application of case enumeration. For simplicity, perform casework on b.

2. If $b = 0$, nothing works, so exclude the case when $b = 0$.

3. Find all a and c for a fixed value of b. Notice that $a \neq 0$. For example, if $b = 1$, then $a + c = 2$, so $(a, c) = (2, 0), (1, 1)$.

4. Add the number of pairs (a, c) for a fixed value of b, found in step 2, by the principle of addition.

2. Bob has two identical-looking bags. In one bag, there are balls numbered 2001 through 2015. In the other bag, there are balls numbered 2016 through 2025. Bob first randomly chooses a bag. Then from that bag, he chooses 3 balls, without replacing the balls between selections. How many different permutation(=ordered arrangement) of 3 balls are possible?

> **Walk-Through**
>
> 1. Notice that there is only 1 way of choosing the first bag, and only 1 way of choosing the second bag.
>
> 2. If the first bag is selected, compute the number of ways to pick out three balls, one at a time.
>
> 3. If the second bag is selected, compute the number of ways to pick out three balls, one at a time.
>
> 4. Thanks to the principle of addition, add the numbers found in step 2 and 3.

3. In a rectangle $ABCD$, $\overline{MN}$ is drawn such that $AM = MB = BC = CN = ND = DA$, and $\overline{MN}$ is parallel to $\overline{AD}$ and $\overline{BC}$. How many *right triangles* can be drawn using any three of the vertices drawn in the figure below?

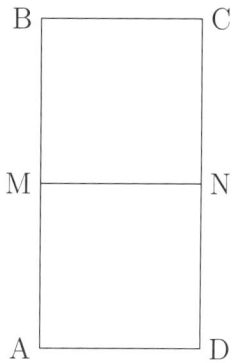

Walk-Through

1. Count the number of right triangles in a square $BCNM$.

2. Count the number of right triangles in a square $NMDA$.

3. Count the number of right triangles in a rectangle $ABCD$.

4. There are more than 4 triangles, well-disguised, in step 3. Geometric count requires careful and thorough inspection.

5. Add the numbers in step 1, 2, and 3.

4. Let $s(x)$ denote the sum of the digits of the positive integer x. For example, $s(10) = 1 + 0 = 1$ and $s(369) = 3 + 6 + 9 = 18$. **For how many values of x that are at most two digits is $s(s(x)) = 3$?**

Walk-Through

1. Paraphrase $s(s(x)) = 3$ into $s(x) = 3, 12, 21, 30, \cdots$.

2. Since $x \leq 99$, it is easy to check $s(x) \leq s(99) = 9 + 9 = 18$. Hence, eliminate the impossible cases found in step 1.

3. Find the values of x for values of $s(x)$ that survived step 2.

4. It is useful to know that integer values of x and $s(x)$ have the same remainder when divided by 9.

5. How many distinct integers are there by multiplying two or more distinct members of the set $\{1, 2, 3, 5, 7\}$?

Walk-Through

1. First, start multiplying two integers from the given set by setting 1 as the smaller of the two.

2. Now, multiply three integers from the set and delete the common ones written in step 1.

3. Multiply four integers from the set and delete the common ones found in step 2.

4. Multiply all five integers and see if the resulting integer appears in the step 3. If it does, then delete it. Otherwise, count it as new.

5. Add all the numbers found in step 1, 2, 3, and 4.

6. The increasing sequence
$$2, 3, 5, 6, 7, 10, \ldots$$
consists of all positive integers which are not perfect squares, cubes, and fourth and fifth powers. What is the 1000th number in this sequence?

Walk-Through

1. This is an application of complementary counting. Let's construct a method of finding the nth integer.

2. Let $n = 6$, and see what happens.

3. Find the perfect squares, cubes, and other powers smaller than or equal to 6.

4. Add the number found in step 3 to $n = 6$ to retrieve 8. Notice that 8 is a perfect cube. So, we move to 9. Notice that 9 is a perfect square. Conclude that 10 is the sixth term.

5. Apply the same logic to $n = 1000$.

6. If there is any perfect power between 1000 and the number found by the steps above, one must delete the perfect power and change the answer by adding the number of perfect powers discussed in this step.

7. The sequence $C = \{2, 3, 5, 6, 7, 10, 11, \ldots\}$ contains all the positive integers from least to greatest that are neither squares nor cubes. If a_n is the nth term of the sequence from least to greatest, find the value of a_{400}.

Walk-Through

1. This is a twin problem to the previous problem. Use the same method to the previous one.

2. Find the perfect squares and cubes smaller than or equal to 400.

3. Add the number found in step 2 to $n = 400$ to retrieve a number.

4. If there is any perfect square or cube between the number found by the steps above and 400, one must delete the perfect square or power and change the answer by adding the number of integers discussed in this step.

8. How many 4-letter words with at least one consonant can be constructed from the letters A, B, C, D, and E? Here, B, C, and D are consonants, any word is valid, and letters may be repeated.

> **Walk-Through**
>
> 1. Construct four places with letters to be filled, i.e, ☐☐☐☐. We are about to fill these four spots with the given letters.
>
> 2. Underline "at least" to notice that complementary counting might be better.
>
> 3. How many 4-letter words with no consonant can be formed?
>
> 4. Find the total number of 4-letter words formed by using A, B, C, D, and E.
>
> 5. Take out the number of 4-letter words without consonants from step 4, and conclude the problem.

9. How many four-digit positive integers have at least one digit that is a 2 or a 3?

> **Walk-Through**
>
> 1. Construct four places with digits to be filled, i.e, ☐☐☐☐. We are about to fill these four spots with digits from 0 to 9.
>
> 2. The condition of having at least one digit that is either 2 or 3 seems too many to count.
>
> 3. Think about the opposite case of having no digit of 2 or 3.
>
> 4. Find the total number of 4-digit positive integers.
>
> 5. Find the total number of 4-digit positive integers not using digits 2 and 3.
>
> 6. Subtract the number found in step 5 from that in step 4, and conclude the problem.

10. How many positive integers less than or equal to 2021 have an *even number of divisors*?

> **Walk-Through**
>
> 1. Think about an integer with an even number of divisors. There are too many to count. For example, consider $12 = 2^2 \cdot 3$. There are $3 \times 2 (= 6)$ number of divisors of 12.
>
> 2. How about an integer with an odd number of divisors? Consider specific properties related to such integer. For example, consider $4 = 2^2$. There are 3 positive divisors of 4. In particular, if $n = p_1^{2q_1} p_2^{2q_2} \cdots p_k^{2q_k}$ for prime $p_1, p_2, \cdots, p_k$, there are $(2q_1+1)(2q_2+1)\cdots(2q_k+1)$ number of divisors of n.
>
> 3. Find all numbers satisfying the properties listed in step 2.
>
> 4. Subtract the number of integers found in step 3 from 2021.

11. In how many ways can a class-president, secretary, and treasurer be chosen from a group of 4 guys and 4 girls and at least one girl and at least one guy holds at least one of those three positions? However, one person can only serve in at most one position.

Walk-Through

1. Let (C, S, T) be a triple of people. Count the total number of triples without restriction.

2. Underline the part "at least one girl and at least one guy." It means that the triple can't be either all guys or all girls.

3. Think about the cases when (C, S, T) are all filled by guys. Make sure these positions must be filled by different people.

4. Likewise, think about the cases when (C, S, T) are all filled by girls satisfying the given condition.

5. Subtract the numbers found in step 3 and 4 from the total number of cases found in step 1.

12. How many three-digit whole numbers are multiples of neither 5 nor 7?

Walk-Through

1. Let A be the set of three-digit whole numbers divisible by 5, and B be the set of three-digit whole numbers divisible by 7.

2. Let $n = 5k$ be the multiple of 5. Use this to find out the size of A. Likewise, let $n = 7q$ be the multiple of 7. Use this to find out the size of B.

3. What goes in $A \cap B$? Use step 2 to write down a number-form that goes in $A \cap B$, and find the size of $A \cap B$.

4. From the set containing three-digit whole numbers, subtract the size of $A \cup B$.

13. *MOUNTPATHS* is nicely spelled out in magnets on the magnetic door. Bob takes two vowels and three consonants and put them in a bag. If the Ts are indistinguishable, how many distinct possible combinations of letters could he put in the bag?

| M | O | U | N | T | P | A | T | H | S |

Walk-Through

1. There are three vowels $\{A, O, U\}$. Other letters are all consonants.

2. The main difficult part of this problem is to decide how to handle Ts. In this case, we use the technique of casework.

3. How many ways are there to choose no T? How many ways are there to choose one T? Or, how many ways are there to choose two Ts?

4. In each case laid out in step 3, choose consonants, respectively, and conclude the problem.

TOPIC 2 Continuing with Combinatorics

14. If there are 3 females and 6 males, and they are to be seated around a round table, the number of configurations with three females seated not adjacent to each other is equal to $k \times 6!$. Find the value of k. (Here, if one configuration is rotated to equal other configuration, the two are considered equal.)

Walk-Through

1. Remember that this problem consists of circular permutation. Let the first female be seated in 1 seat.

2. Other people would sit down in seats respective to the first female.

3. The value of k must correspond to the number of seats for two other females.

4. With respect to the first female, all seats are fixed. Make sure other females be seated in the remaining seats by fixing one seat to the first female.

5. 6! corresponds to the number of arranging males in the remaining seats. Hence, solve for k and conclude the problem.

15. Given a 50 card deck with cards numbered from 1 through 10 in each of 5 suits - $\alpha, \beta, \gamma, \delta,$ and ϵ. In other words, there are five 1's, i.e., $1_\alpha, 1_\beta, 1_\gamma, 1_\delta$ and 1_ϵ. If there are n 5-card hands that contain exactly one pair of two cards with equal numerical value, compute the value of $\dfrac{n}{5^5}$. (Here, the order of selection does not matter.)

Walk-Through

1. Choose the rank that will be selected as a pair.

2. Choose three ranks that will appear exactly once.

3. Choose two suits that will appear in a pair.

4. Choose one suit for each rank that will appear once.

5. Multiply all numbers from step 1 to 4 to retrieve the value of n.

16. In how many different ways can 3 male dogs and 4 female dogs be placed into two groups of two dogs and one group of three dogs if there must be at least one male and one female in each group? Here, the groups with equal number of dogs are indistinguishable.

| Walk-Through |

1. Partition four female dogs into $\{F, F\}, \{F\}, \{F\}$. There is no order between the second group and the third group because they have the same number of dogs in each group. Make sure to get rid of orders.

2. Each of the male dogs chooses a group with female dog(s). This is no longer partition. This is more of a permutation of three dogs in three different places.

3. Multiply the numbers found in step 1 and 2.

17. Suppose there are 12 students with 6 boys and 6 girls. The class president must divide the students into three groups and he has 4 hats in white, gold and magenta to mark the three teams for baseball. If each team has at least one girl and at least one boy, how many ways can he give out the hats? Here, hats of equal color are not distinct.

Walk-Through

1. Consider two cases in total.

2. The first case is $(b, b, g, g), (b, b, g, g), (b, b, g, g)$. Find the number of ways of partitioning boys into three groups with two members each and sending girls to the groups with two boys each.

3. The second case is $(b, b, b, g), (b, b, g, g), (b, g, g, g)$. Find the number of ways of partitioning boys into three groups with three, two and one member each, and sending girls to the groups, respectively.

4. For the groups in step 2 and 3, make sure hats with different colors are assigned.

5. Add numbers found in step 4 to conclude the problem.

18. Notice that $9 = 2^2 + 2^2 + 2^0$. How many distinguishable ways are there to write 9 as the sum of 2^0, 2^1, and 2^2, where the order of how they add matters? For example, $1+4+4$, $4+1+4$, and $4+4+1$ are considered all distinct.

> **Walk-Through**
>
> 1. This uses the technique of casework - comprehensive and exhaustive.
>
> 2. Use as many 4s as possible.
>
> 3. Without using 4s, use as many 2s as possible.
>
> 4. Without using 4s and 1s, use as many 1s as possible.
>
> 5. Arrange each of the tuples found in step 2, 3, and 4. Add the number of different tuples found in this step to conclude the problem.

19. Bob, a notoriously genius mathlete, has 5 pieces of quiz sets, each with different math problems. In how many ways can he give these quiz sets to his 10 friends, where each friend can receive more than one quiz set?

Walk-Through

1. Count the number of ways that the first quiz is assigned.

2. Count the number of ways that the second quiz is assigned.

3. Keep continuing this process until the last quiz is assigned.

4. Multiply the number of ways found in step 1, 2, and 3, to conclude the problem.

5. Notice what 5^{10} means, in terms of quiz sets and Bob's friends.

20. At the grocery store, I bought 4 different items. I brought 3 identical-looking bags, and handed them to the cashier. How many ways are there for the cashier to put the items I bought in the 3 identical-looking bags, assuming he might leave some of the bags empty?

> **Walk-Through**
>
> 1. Underline "identical-looking." It means that you should fix the order.
>
> 2. Let a, b, and c the number of items in bags such that $a \geq b \geq c$.
>
> 3. Set up the equation $a + b + c = 4$ where $a \geq b \geq c$.
>
> 4. This shows all triples satisfying natural partition.
>
> 5. We borrow these set-ups for partition of sets (or committee selection).
>
> 6. Make sure if there are groups with the same number of members, we divide by the number of possible arrangement.
>
> 7. This problem is a classic example of "committee selection."

21. How many ways are there to put 5 balls in 3 boxes if the balls are distinguishable but the boxes are not?

> **Walk-Through**
>
> 1. This is a twin question of the previous problem.
>
> 2. Let x, y, and z be non-negative integers such that $x \geq y \geq z$.
>
> 3. Set up an equation $x + y + z = 5$ where $x \geq y \geq z$.
>
> 4. For all triples, we borrow the structure of these triples for committee selection.
>
> 5. Make sure you divide by the number of possible arrangements for groups with the same number of items. For instance, if $x + y + z = 2 + 2 + 1$, then there are $\frac{\binom{5}{2}\binom{3}{2}\binom{1}{1}}{2!}$, since there are two groups with the same number of members.

TOPIC 2 Continuing with Combinatorics

22. Bob likes coffee a lot. He can scoop coffee bean with a steel scoop from a tray with Hawaiian Kona beans, Jamaican blue mountain beans, and Tanzanian peaberry beans. There are enough beans at each tray with at least six scoops. How many different assortments of six scoops of coffee bean can be selected? (Note that coffee bean scoops of the same type are not distinguishable, and assume that steel scoop can take out equal amount of bean every time.)

Walk-Through

1. This is a classic problem of "combination allowing repetition" or "circles and bars"(or stars-and-bars).

2. Let a, b, and c be non-negative integers such that $a \geq b \geq c$.

3. Set up an equation $a + b + c = 6$ where $a \geq b \geq c \geq 0$.

4. Arrange each triple for different variations.

5. Think about how the total count has one-to-one correspondence with circles-and-bars. Try to reason why the total count has the same structure as $\binom{8}{2}$.

23. Bob's little brother, Bo, has 7 identical stickers and 4 identical sheets of paper. How many ways are there for him to put all of the stickers on the sheets of paper, if only the number of stickers on each sheet matters?

> **Walk-Through**
>
> 1. This is a classic problem of partition of natural numbers.
>
> 2. Let a, b, c, and d be non-negative integers such that $a \geq b \geq c \geq d \geq 0$.
>
> 3. Set up an equation $a + b + c + d = 7$ where $a \geq b \geq c \geq d \geq 0$.
>
> 4. Do not arrange each triple for different variations. Simply find all quadruples satisfying the given condition.

24. If a, b, and c are integers such that $1 \leq a \leq b \leq c \leq 3$, in how many ways can all triples of (a, b, c) be written?

Walk-Through

1. One can solve this using casework.

2. Assume that $a = b = c$. Find the number of triples satisfying the given assumption.

3. Assume that $a = b < c$. Find the number of triples satisfying the given assumption.

4. Assume that $a < b = c$. Find the number of triples satisfying the given assumption.

5. Assume that $a < b < c$. Find the number of triples satisfying the given assumption.

6. Add all numbers found in the previous steps.

7. Try understand why circles-and-bars may solve this problem.

25. If $a + b < 10$ for non-negative integers a and b, in how many ways can all possible pairs of (a, b) be written?

> **Walk-Through**
>
> 1. This is a classic problem of hockey-stick identity.
>
> 2. Solve for the number of pairs satisfying $a + b = 9, 8, 7, 6, \cdots, 0$.
>
> 3. Express each number as a binomial coefficient.
>
> 4. Notice that the sum of binomial coefficients equals another binomial coefficient, according to the hockey-stick identity.
>
> 5. What if you try introducing another variable c such that $a+b+c = 9$? Do we get the same value?

Answer Key

1. 45

We can perform caseworks on b. If $b = 1$, there are 2 possibilities for (a, c). If $b = 2$, there are 4 possibilities. If $b = 3$, then there are 6 possibilities. If $b = 4$, there are 8 possibilities. If $b = 5$, there are 9 possibilities. Likewise, if $b = 6$, there are 7 possibilities. The process goes onward, until $b = 9$. There are 45 possible numbers.

2. 3450

If he chooses the first bag, there are $15 \times 14 \times 13$ possibilities. Likewise, if he chooses the second bag, there are $10 \times 9 \times 8$ possibilities. Hence, the number of different ordered selections must be 3450.

3. 14

Choose two points from the side $\overline{AB}$ and one point from the side $\overline{CD}$, i.e., $\binom{3}{2} \times \binom{3}{1} = 9$. Likewise, choose two points from the side $\overline{CD}$ and one point from the side $\overline{AB}$, i.e., $\binom{3}{1} \times \binom{3}{2} = 9$. Hence, there are 18 possible triangles formed, since triangles BMD, AMC, DNB and CNA are all non-right triangles, we eliminate four possible triangles. Hence, the answer must be 14.

4. 11

Since $s(s(x)) = 3$, we get $s(x) = 3, 12, 21,$ and 30. Hence, $x = 3, 12, 21, 30$ and $39, 48, 57, \cdots, 93$. Thus we get 11 values of x.

5. 15

The question is asking us about the number of distinct divisors of $2 \times 3 \times 5 \times 7$. However, 1 should be excluded. Hence, there are 15 such numbers.

6. 1041

First, compute the number of perfect squares smaller than or equal to 1000. There are 31 numbers. There are 7 perfect cubes except the ones overcounted. Perfect fourth powers are all excluded from perfect squares. There are 2 perfect fifth powers. Hence, $1000 + 40 = 1040$ seems to be the right answer. However, $1024 = 2^{10}$ is a number between 1000 and 1040. Therefore, we skip one number to the right. The answer must be 1041.

7. 425

Follow the same strategy in the previous question. Compute the number of all squares less than or equal to 400. There are 20 such numbers. Compute the number of all cubes less than or equal to 400. There are 5 numbers excluding the squares. Hence, the number must be 425. Thankfully, there is no perfect squares nor perfect cubes between 400 and 425, so there is no need to skip a number.

8. 609

Use complementary counting.

$$5^4 - 2^4 = 609$$

78   The Essential Guide to **Competition Math**(Fundamentals Plus)

9. 5416

Out of 9×10^3 possible four-digit numbers, we eliminate 7×8^3 possible numbers. Hence, the answer must be 5416.

10. 1977

An integer with odd number of divisors is a perfect square. Therefore, eliminate 44 perfect squares from 2021. The answer must be 1977.

11. 288

Out of total possibilities, we compute the possible cases when there are all guys or girls picked. Hence,
$8 \cdot 7 \cdot 6 - 2(4 \cdot 3 \cdot 2) = 288$ cases are the answer.

12. 618

From 100 to 995, there are 180 multiples of 5. From 105 to 994, there are 128 multiples of 7. From 105 to 980, there are 26 multiples of 35. Hence,
$900 - (180 + 128 - 26) = 618$ is the answer.

13. 75

There are $\binom{3}{2}$ ways to choose two vowels. For consonants, perform caseworks. If there is 0 T, there are $\binom{5}{3} = 10$ ways to choose three consonants. If there is 1 T, there are $\binom{5}{2} = 10$ ways to choose the three. If there are 2 T's, there are $\binom{5}{1} = 5$ ways to choose the three. Therefore, $3 \times 25 = 75$ is the answer.

14. 20

For the first female. Let her choose the spot. There are 1 way for her to choose the seat. Then, let a, b, and c be the number of seats between the first female and second female, second and third, and third and first, respectively. Then, we are solving for $a + b + c = 6$ where $a, b, c \geq 1$. This is a typical example of combination allowing repetitions. Hence, there are $\binom{5}{2} = 10$ ways to choose seats for males, and second and third female may change their seats. Therefore, there are $20 \times 6!$ possible ways. The answer must be 20.

15. 336

Use combination properly.
$$n = 10 \times \binom{9}{3} \times 5^3 \times \binom{5}{2}$$

Hence, $\dfrac{n}{5^5} = 336$.

16. 36

Partition four female dogs first.
$$\dfrac{\binom{4}{2} \times \binom{2}{1} \times \binom{1}{1}}{2!}$$

Then, multiply 3! for the male dogs to choose the groups. Hence, there are 36 possible configurations.

17. 29700

Either $\binom{6}{3} \times \binom{3}{2} \times \binom{1}{1} \times \binom{6}{3} \times \binom{3}{1} \times \binom{2}{2} \times 3!$
or $\dfrac{\binom{6}{2} \times \binom{4}{2} \times \binom{2}{2}}{3!} \times \binom{6}{2} \times \binom{4}{2} \times \binom{2}{2} \times 3!$.
Hence, there are 29700 configurations.

18. 96

First, partition 9 into natural numbers.

$$9 = 4 + 4 + 1$$
$$= 4 + 2 + 2 + 1$$
$$= 4 + 2 + 1 + 1 + 1$$
$$= 4 + 1 + 1 + 1 + 1 + 1$$
$$= 2 + 2 + 2 + 2 + 1$$
$$= 2 + 2 + 2 + 1 + 1 + 1$$
$$= 2 + 2 + 1 + 1 + 1 + 1 + 1$$
$$= 2 + 1 + 1 + 1 + 1 + 1 + 1 + 1$$
$$= 1 + 1 + \cdots + 1$$

Then, put orders.

$$\frac{3!}{2!} + \frac{4!}{2!} + \frac{5!}{4!} + \frac{5!}{3!} + \frac{6!}{5!} + \frac{7!}{5!2!} + 8 + 1$$

There are 96 possible configurations.

19. 100000

Each quiz has 10 possible number of students to choose. Hence, 10^5 is the answer, not 5^{10}.

20. 14

$$x + y + z = 4$$
$$4 + 0 + 0 = 4$$
$$3 + 1 + 0 = 4$$
$$2 + 2 + 0 = 4$$
$$2 + 1 + 1 = 4$$

Now, take four partitions of sets. We get $\binom{4}{4}$, $\binom{4}{3}\binom{1}{1}$, $\frac{\binom{4}{2}\binom{2}{2}}{2!}$ and $\frac{\binom{4}{2}\binom{2}{1}\binom{1}{1}}{2!}$, so the answer is 14.

21. 41

$$x + y + z = 5$$
$$5 + 0 + 0 = 5$$
$$4 + 1 + 0 = 5$$
$$3 + 2 + 0 = 5$$
$$3 + 1 + 1 = 5$$
$$2 + 2 + 1 = 5$$

There are five different possible partitions of 5 into three non-negative numbers. Now take this into partition of sets. Hence, the answer must be the sum of $\binom{5}{5}$, $\binom{5}{4}\binom{1}{1}$, $\binom{5}{3}\binom{2}{2}$, $\binom{5}{3}\frac{\binom{2}{1}\binom{1}{1}}{2!}$, and $\frac{\binom{5}{2}\binom{3}{2}}{2!}\binom{1}{1}$, i.e., 41.

22. 28

This is a typical type of combination allowing repetition. Let a, b, and c, be the number of scoops of each coffee beans respectively. Then, $a + b + c = 6$, allowing 0's for a, b, and c. Hence, the answer is $\binom{8}{2} = 28$.

23. 11

Simply take a partition of 7 into four non-negative numbers. If $a + b + c + d = 7$, where we allow non-negative integers, we get (a, b, c, d) as $(7, 0, 0, 0)$, $(6, 1, 0, 0)$, $(5, 2, 0, 0)$, $(4, 3, 0, 0)$, $(5, 1, 1, 0)$, $(4, 2, 1, 0)$, $(3, 3, 1, 0)$, $(3, 2, 2, 0)$, $(4, 1, 1, 1)$, $(3, 2, 1, 1)$ and $(2, 2, 2, 1)$. Therefore, there are 11 possible configurations.

24. 10

Let α be the number of 1's that appeared, β that of 2's that appeared, and γ that of 3's that appeared. Hence, $\alpha + \beta + \gamma = 3$ where non-negative integers are allowed. Thus, the answer is $\binom{5}{2} = 10$.

25. 55

Instead of solving inequality. Introduce a new variable c such that $a + b < 10$ implies $a + b + c = 9$ where a, b, and c can be non-negative integers. Thus, we find all possible values of (a, b) by using combination allowing repetition. The answer must be $\binom{11}{2} = 55$.

 # Quotes from Mathematicans

"The only way to learn mathematics is to do mathematics." - Paul Halmos

"In mathematics, the art of proposing a question must be held of higher value than solving it." - Georg Cantor

"Mathematics is not about numbers, equations, computations, or algorithms: it is about understanding." - William Paul Thurston

"It is not enough to have a good mind; the main thing is to use it well." - René Descartes

"The essence of mathematics lies in its freedom." - Georg Cantor

"In mathematics, the truth is somewhere out there in a place no one knows, beyond all the beaten paths. And it is worth seeking." - Yōko Ogawa

"Mathematics, rightly viewed, possesses not only truth but supreme beauty." - Bertrand Russell

"Mathematics is the most beautiful and most powerful creation of the human spirit." - Stefan Banach

"Mathematics is the language in which God has written the universe." - Galileo Galilei

TOPIC 3

Ending with Combinatorics

3.1 Probability with Restrictions

3.2 More about Probability

3.3 Practices

3.1 Probability with Restrictions

Probability is a proportion of a specific event over the total number of events. How do we normally calculate probability with restrictions? This is equivalent to count with multiple conditions. All we need to do is to count the total number of events and the number of specific events. Let's have a look at the following example.

Example What is the probability that a two-digit integer has its unit digit as 3 or 7?

Solution First of all, let's compute the total number of two-digit numbers. Using the counting principle, we may say there are 9×10 two-digit numbers. Now, the specific numbers you may wish to find is $\overline{A3}$ or $\overline{A7}$ where A is a tens-digit number. Hence, we get $9 \times 2 = 18$ two-digit numbers satisfying the given condition. On the other hand, you can argue with the principle of multiplication of probability, i.e.,

$$\frac{9}{9} \times \frac{2}{10} = \frac{18}{90} = \frac{1}{5}$$

When we multiply probabilities directly, we should be extra careful of what we multiply or not. Specifically, if we are multiplying by the same kinds or distinct kinds, we may have different answers.

Example Given a fair 6-sided die, what is the probability of having one even and one odd in two throws?

Solution The first thing we do is to get the first-hand idea. I would like to pick even first, then odd last. In that case, the probability must be

$$\frac{3}{6} \times \frac{3}{6}$$

However, in the question, there is no phrase about picking even first. You must consider the case when odd number gets picked first. Hence, we multiply by two possibilities, i.e., (even,odd) and (odd,even), in the end. Therefore, the answer must be $1/2$.

Example Given a fair 6-sided die, what is the probability of having two even faces in two throws?

Solution Picking two even numbers does not require you to think about the choice order. In other words, you just pick one even number and another even one. Hence, the probability is

$$\frac{3}{6} \times \frac{3}{6} = \frac{1}{4}$$

Oftentimes, it is best to think about the probability tree. AMC style questions may combine recursions and probability, so you must be good at counting cases that satisfy the given condition using the probability tree. Let's have a look at the following example.

Example Suppose there are five people seated in a round table. If each person flips a coin, what is the probability that no two adjacent people have both heads?

Solution We case-enumerate. Pick anyone, calling him the 0th person, and we will count all possible cases by clockwise rotation. If he or she flips heads, the 1st person must have tails. Then, the 2nd person must have heads/tails. The 3rd person must have either tails, or heads/tails. The 4th person must have either heads/<u>tails</u>, <u>tails</u>, or heads/<u>tails</u>, respectively. Hence, there are 3 possible cases if the 0th person has heads. On the other hand, if 0th person has (tails), then the 1st person has (heads/tails), 2nd person (tails, heads/tails), 3rd person (heads/tails, tails, heads/tails), and 4th person (tails, heads/tails, heads/tails, tails, heads/tails). Therefore, there are 8 possible cases. In total, there are 11 possible cases depending on whether the 0th person has heads or tails. Thus, the probability is

$$\frac{3+8}{2^5} = \frac{11}{32}$$

This is a classic example of Fibonacci sequence. Consider the following diagram to see why this recurrence relation is Fibonacci.

$$H \to \mathbf{T} \to H/\mathbf{T} \to \mathbf{T}, H/\mathbf{T} \to H/\mathbf{T}, \mathbf{T}, H/\mathbf{T}$$

Can you see $0, 1, 1, 2, 3$? This is a Fibonacci sequence. Think about the second case as well.

$$T \to H/T \to T, H/T \to H/T, T, H/T \to T, H/T, H/T, T, H/T$$

We get $1, 2, 3, 5, 8$, which is indeed Fibonacci. As we write down probability tree for taking conditions into account and we usually get Fibonacci sequence, you may safely assume that you are solving the question correctly.

3.2 More about Probability

As you learned in the previous topic, partition of sets requires you to use combination. In fact, combination is used oftentimes in probability. Combination, unlike permutation, does not care about the order. You have to be careful about "not caring about the order." In fact, combination has only one order. All different arrangements are discarded as overcounts. This is pretty much equal to the permutation with repeated letters as well.

Example Find all possible arrangements of $AABBB$.

Solution First solution we may think of is to consider $A_1 A_2 B_1 B_2 B_3$, all distinct. Then, we get permutation of five letters. However, since (A_1, A_2), (A_2, A_1) are in fact equal to one another, we have to get rid of the overcounts. Likewise, (B_1, B_2, B_3), (B_1, B_3, B_2), (B_2, B_1, B_3), (B_2, B_3, B_1), (B_3, B_1, B_2) and (B_3, B_2, B_1) should be considered all equal, we have to divide the total counts by 6. Hence, the answer is

$$\frac{5!}{2!3!}$$

Second solution we may consider is finding proper positions. Suppose there are five spots in an array, i.e., $\square\square\square\square\square$. Choose two spots for A, so we get $\binom{5}{2}$. Automatically, all three spots will be filled by B's. Hence, the answer must be $\binom{5}{2} = \frac{5!}{2!3!}$.

Now, let's talk about Bayesian probability, particularly useful in situations where prior knowledge or evidence needs to be combined with new information to make informed decisions. Bayes' Theorem is the foundation of Bayesian probability. It allows us to update the probability of a hypothesis H given new evidence E. The theorem is expressed as:

$$P(H|E) = \frac{P(E|H) \cdot P(H)}{P(E)}$$

where:

- $P(H|E)$ is the **posterior probability**, the probability of the hypothesis H given the evidence E.

- $P(E|H)$ is the **likelihood**, the probability of observing the evidence E given that the hypothesis H is true.

- $P(H)$ is the **prior probability**, the initial probability of the hypothesis H before observing the evidence.

- $P(E)$ is the **marginal probability** of the evidence E, which can be computed as the sum of the probabilities of E under all possible hypotheses.

Example Consider a scenario where a doctor is trying to diagnose a patient for a specific disease D. The doctor knows the following information.

- The prior probability $P(D)$ of having the disease, based on general population statistics.

- The likelihood $P(\text{positive test}|D)$, the probability that a patient with the disease tests positive.

- The probability $P(\text{positive test})$ that a randomly selected patient tests positive, regardless of whether they have the disease.

Given a positive test result, the doctor can use Bayes' Theorem to update the probability that the patient has the disease:

$$P(D|\text{positive test}) = \frac{P(\text{positive test}|D) \cdot P(D)}{P(\text{positive test})}$$

Example Suppose there is a factory that produces two types of widgets: Type A and Type B. The factory produces 60% Type A widgets and 40% Type B widgets. The quality control department knows that 5% of Type A widgets and 10% of Type B widgets are defective. If a randomly selected widget is found to be defective, what is the probability that it is a Type B widget?

Solution We can use Bayes' Theorem to solve this problem. Let's write down what has been provided.

- $P(A) = 0.60$ (the prior probability that a widget is of Type A).

- $P(B) = 0.40$ (the prior probability that a widget is of Type B).

- $P(D|A) = 0.05$ (the probability that a Type A widget is defective).

- $P(D|B) = 0.10$ (the probability that a Type B widget is defective).

We want to find the probability $P(B|D)$, the probability that a widget is of Type B given that it is defective. First, we calculate the total probability that a widget is defective, $P(D)$, using the law of total probability:

$$P(D) = (0.05 \times 0.60) + (0.10 \times 0.40) = 0.03 + 0.04 = 0.07$$

Next, we apply Bayes' Theorem to find $P(B|D)$:

$$P(B|D) = \frac{0.10 \times 0.40}{0.07} = \frac{0.04}{0.07} \approx 0.571$$

3.3 Practices

1. Four fair six-sided dice are rolled at a time. Given that the product of their values is even, what is the probability that their sum is odd?

> **Walk-Through**
>
> 1. This is a typical conditional probability. Let B be the number of events when the product of face-values is even.
>
> 2. Let A be the number of events when the sum of face-values is odd.
>
> 3. We must find $p(A|B)$, which is defined as $\frac{p(A \cap B)}{p(B)}$.
>
> 4. Since this is a probability problem, order matters. In fact, we would get the same answer when order does not matter. Hence, assume that order matters for simplicity.

2. If the integers a and b are randomly selected, where $-2 \leq a \leq 5$ and $2 \leq b \leq 7$, what is the probability that a is divisible by b?

Walk-Through

1. Perform case-works for the values of a.

2. Find all possible values of b for $a = -2, -1, 0, 1, 2, \cdots, 5$.

3. Add the number of values of b found in step 2.

4. Divide the number found in step 3 by the total number of ordered pairs (a, b).

3. Assume that three cards are dealt at random from a standard deck of 52 cards with four suits, each of which contains 13 cards. What is the probability that the first card is a 3, the second card is a $\diamond$, and the third card is an Ace?

> **Walk-Through**
>
> 1. This can easily be solved by tree-diagram.
>
> 2. Assume the first is $3\diamond$ or $3*$ where $*$ is a non-diamond.
>
> 3. Assume the second is $1\diamond$ or $X\diamond$ where X is non-1.
>
> 4. Assume the third is $1*$ where $*$ is any suit.
>
> 5. There are four possible tree-nodes. Compute the sum of all possible values in each node.

4. Assume there is a bag containing two red marbles and two blue marbles, and more than four red marbles outside the bag. As soon as a marble is randomly pulled out, it is automatically replaced with a red marble regardless of its color that is pulled out. What is the probability that all *marbles in the bag* are red after three such replacements?

> **Walk-Through**
>
> 1. Draw a tree-diagram that fits the given situation.
>
> 2. There are three possible cases, each of which has different probability value.
>
> 3. Compute the sum of three cases to conclude solving the problem.

5. A card is chosen at random from a standard deck of 52 cards, and then it is replaced and another card is chosen. What is the probability that at least one of the cards is a diamond or a king?

> **Walk-Through**
>
> 1. Underline "at least." This calls out for complementary probability.
>
> 2. Find the probability that no card is neither diamond nor king.
>
> 3. Since the cards neither diamond nor king are of equal kinds, we do not multiply by any possible permutation of the cards.
>
> 4. Subtract the probability found in step 2 from 1.

6. If Bob rolls six fair 6-sided dice at once, what is the probability that at least two dice share equal numerical face value?

> **Walk-Through**
>
> 1. Underline "at least." This calls out for complementary probability.
>
> 2. Find the probability that no card shares face value.
>
> 3. Subtract the probability found in step 2 from 1.

7. If five fair 6-sided dice are rolled, what is the probability that at most four of them will show a 6?

> **Walk-Through**
>
> 1. Underline "at most." The complementary case is when there are five 6's.
>
> 2. Find the probability that no card shares face value.
>
> 3. Subtract the probability found in step 2 from 1.

8. Bob visited his family at New York during Christmas break and stayed at a 3rd floor single-room at a 30-story hotel, and he was bored due to the quarantine he had to make for COVID-19. So, he decided to play a game where he gets inside an elevator on his floor. He flips a fair coin five times to determine his next five stops. Each time he flips heads, he goes up one floor. Each time he flips tails, he goes down one floor. What is the probability that every stop is above his room floor?

Walk-Through

1. Draw a tree-diagram.

2. Notice that Bob must go up a certain number of steps for the first few times to satisfy the given condition.

3. Count the total number of cases that match the condition.

4. Divide the number found in step 3 from the total number of cases.

9. Two fair six-sided dice are rolled. What is the probability that the product of the two numbers is a composite number?

Walk-Through

1. A positive integer may be either 1, prime, or composite number.

2. Notice that one may solve this using direct counting or complementary counting. In this walk-through, we choose complementary counting.

3. Compute the number of cases when the product of two face-values is 1 or prime.

4. Subtract the number found in step 3 from the total number of cases.

5. Divide the number found in step 3 by the total number of cases.

10. Alice and Bob each choose a whole number randomly between 1 and 10, inclusive. What is the probability that the product of their numbers is more than 10?

Walk-Through

1. One may solve this by direct counting or complementary counting. In this walk-through, choose complementary counting.

2. Let a and b be whole numbers chosen by Alice and Bob, respectively.

3. Perform casework for a such that $ab \leq 10$.

4. Or, perform casework for $ab \leq 10$ where $ab = 10, 9, 8, \cdots 1$.

5. From the total number of ordered pairs (a, b), subtract the number found in either step 3 or 4.

6. Divide the number found in step 5 by the total number of ordered pairs (a, b).

11. Denice and Janice each choose a number, not necessarily distinct, at random from the first six primes, i.e., $\{2, 3, 5, 7, 11, 13\}$. What is the probability that the sum of the numbers they choose is even?

> **Walk-Through**
>
> 1. Let D and J be the number that Denice and Janice choose, respectively.
>
> 2. Think about parity. Adding two even integers is even. Likewise, adding two odd integers is even.
>
> 3. Remember there is only one even prime.
>
> 4. Find all cases that satisfy the condition laid in step 2. Divide it by the total number of ordered pairs (D, J).

12. A special game consists of rolling a standard die and tossing a fair coin. Each turn, a die is rolled and a coin is tossed. The game is won at a particular turn if the die shows a 2 or a 3 and the coin shows tails. What is the probability that the game will be won before the fourth turn?

> **Walk-Through**
>
> 1. Let p be the probability of winning the game.
>
> 2. The problem asks for the case when the game is won before the fourth turn, so it must be won either the first turn, second turn, or third turn.
>
> 3. Find the probability when the game is won in the first turn.
>
> 4. Find the probability when the game is won in the second turn, not in the first turn.
>
> 5. Find the probability when the game is won in the third turn, not in the first or second turn.
>
> 6. Add all probabilities listed in step 3, 4, and 5.

13. Bob has three types of imaginary bills - 25-dollar bill, 5-dollar bill and 1-dollar bill - where he has three of each kind. If Bob selects three bills at random at a time without replacement, what is the probability that the sum of monetary values is other than 35 dollars?

> **Walk-Through**
>
> 1. Let p be the probability that the sum of monetary values is exactly 35 dollars.
>
> 2. Choose one 25 dollar bill, and two 5 dollar bills.
>
> 3. Since choosing different kinds, order matters. In other words, multiply by 3 to a specific probability of your preferred order.

14. If three cards are chosen at random from a standard 52-card deck, what is the probability that two of the cards match in rank yet the third card is different in rank?

> **Walk-Through**
>
> 1. Use constructive probability.
>
> 2. Choose the rank that appears twice.
>
> 3. Choose the rank that appears once.
>
> 4. Choose the suits for the ranks that appear twice.
>
> 5. Choose the suit for the rank that appear once.
>
> 6. Divide by the total number of selections of three cards.

15. What is the probability that a randomly selected factor of 70^{11} is a multiple of 70^6?

> **Walk-Through**
>
> 1. Prime factorize 70^{11}.
>
> 2. Understand the meaning of "a multiple of 70^6" in terms of prime factors.
>
> 3. Find the number of exponents one can choose for powers of 2.
>
> 4. Find the number of exponents one can choose for powers of 5.
>
> 5. Find the number of exponents one can choose for powers of 7.
>
> 6. Use step 3, 4, and 5 to conclude the problem.

16. If three fair six-sided dice are to be rolled, what is the probability that the product of the top faces' numbers is prime?

> **Walk-Through**
>
> 1. Let (a, b, c) be the number of possible triples formed by rolling three fair six-sided dice.
>
> 2. One of the entries should be prime, while others should be 1. In particular, $(a, b, c) = (1, 1, P)$, $(1, P, 1)$ or $(P, 1, 1)$. Try to reason why these three possibilities are considered distinct in this problem.
>
> 3. Remember there are three prime face-values in each die.
>
> 4. Conclude the problem by using the principle of multiplication for probability.

17. Suppose a and b are distinct integers between 1 and 50, inclusive. What is the probability that $ab + a + b$ is one less than a multiple of 5?

> **Walk-Through**
>
> 1. Label the expression "one less than a multiple of 5," i.e., $5k - 1$.
>
> 2. Write $ab + a + b = 5k - 1$.
>
> 3. Rewrite it into $ab + a + b + 1 = 5k$.
>
> 4. Think about Simon's Favorite Factoring Technique.
>
> 5. Now, consider three possible case-works on (a, b), and conclude solving the problem.

18. If forty cards are placed into a box, each with a whole number 1 through 10, where the number is written on four cards each, let p the probability that three of the cards bear the same number while the other one bears a different number. If $p = \dfrac{m}{n}$ where m and n are relatively prime, find the value of m.

$$\boxed{1}\,\boxed{1}\,\boxed{1}\,\boxed{1}\,\boxed{2}\,\boxed{2}\,\boxed{2}\,\boxed{2}\,\cdots\,\boxed{10}\,\boxed{10}\,\boxed{10}\,\boxed{10}$$

Walk-Through

1. Use constructive probability.

2. Choose a number that appears three times.

3. Choose a number that appears once.

4. Multiply by the probability in your preferred order.

5. Knowing that this contains a mixture of different kinds, multiply by the number of arrangements of three identical-looking cards and one different card.

19. If five fair six-sided dice is rolled once at a time, what is the probability that there is at least a pair but not a triple? In other words, there are two dice with the same numerical value, but no three dice with the same value. For instance, we should count $(1,1,2,2,3)$ or $(1,1,2,3,4)$, but not $(1,1,1,2,2)$.

Walk-Through

1. Use constructive probability.

2. There are two cases to consider to solve this problem.

3. The first case must be the type of choosing $\boxed{1}\,\boxed{1}\,\boxed{2}\,\boxed{2}\,\boxed{3}$, for instance.

4. The second case must be the type of choosing $\boxed{1}\,\boxed{1}\,\boxed{2}\,\boxed{3}\,\boxed{4}$, for instance.

5. Repeat the same procedure covered in the previous problem.

20. If three female students and six male students are to be seated around the round table, what is the probability that female students are never adjacent to each other and the number of male students between two female students is distinct?

> **Walk-Through**
>
> 1. Let the first female be seated.
>
> 2. Other people may be seated in 8! different ways, which is the total count for this set-up.
>
> 3. Now, label all eight seats in a fixed order from left to right from the first female's perspective.
>
> 4. Count the total number of ways that other two females be seated, satisfying the given condition in the problem.
>
> 5. Divide the number found in step 4 by step 2.

TOPIC 3 Ending with Combinatorics 107

21. If Bob rolls four fair six-sided dice, what is the probability that he rolls more 5s than 6s?

Walk-Through

1. Use complementary probability.

2. Let p be the probability that he rolls more 5s than 6s. Then, this must be the same probability that he rolls more 6s than 5s, thanks to symmetry. Hence, let q be the probability that he rolls the same number of 5s as that of 6s.

3. Compute q in step 4, 5, and 6.

4. First, find the probability when there is no 5 nor 6.

5. Second, find the probability when there are one 5 and one 6.

6. Third, find the probability when there are two 5s and two 6s.

7. Find the sum of step 4, 5, and 6, i.e., the value of q.

8. Subtract q from 1, and divide it by 2 to conclude solving the problem.

22. If forty cards are placed into a box, each with a whole number 1 through 10, where the number is written on four cards each, the probability of picking up four distinct cards such that two of the cards have the same numerical value while the other two bear equal values as well can be written as $\dfrac{a \cdot b \cdot c}{p \cdot q \cdot r}$ in lowest term, where p, q, and r are prime numbers, and a, b and c in rearranged order are consecutive multiples of 3. What is the value of $p + q + r$?

$$\boxed{1}\,\boxed{1}\,\boxed{1}\,\boxed{1}\,\boxed{2}\,\boxed{2}\,\boxed{2}\,\boxed{2}\,\cdots\,\boxed{10}\,\boxed{10}\,\boxed{10}\,\boxed{10}$$

Walk-Through

1. Use constructive probability.

2. Let's use letters and symbols for simplicity. Let $\boxed{A}\,\boxed{A}\,\boxed{B}\,\boxed{B}$ be one example of four-card selection.

3. Choose a number that goes in A.

4. Choose another number that goes in B.

5. There should be no order between step 3 and 4, because the order formed by arranging the cards will be multiplied in step 7.

6. Find the specific probability of choosing $\boxed{A}\,\boxed{A}\,\boxed{B}\,\boxed{B}$, in the written order.

7. Now, multiply by the number of arrangements of $\boxed{A}\,\boxed{A}\,\boxed{B}\,\boxed{B}$.

8. Retrieve the values of a, b, c, p, q, and r, and conclude solving the problem.

23. Bob has eight socks, two of each color: black, brown, white, and green. He randomly draws four socks. What is the probability that he has exactly one pair of socks with the same color?

> **Walk-Through**
>
> 1. Use constructive probability.
>
> 2. Let $\boxed{A}\,\boxed{A}\,\boxed{B}\,\boxed{C}$ be one particular example of selecting socks.
>
> 3. Choose the color that appears twice. In other words, choose the color that goes inside $\boxed{A}$.
>
> 4. Choose the color that appears in $\boxed{B}$.
>
> 5. Choose the color that appears in $\boxed{C}$.
>
> 6. Make sure there is no order between step 4 and 5, for the order of arrangements will be multiplied in step 7.
>
> 7. Find the specific probability for $\boxed{A}\,\boxed{A}\,\boxed{B}\,\boxed{C}$, in the written order.
>
> 8. Multiply by the number of arrangements for $\boxed{A}\,\boxed{A}\,\boxed{B}$ and $\boxed{C}$, and conclude solving the problem.

24. What is the probability that Bob gets more heads than tails if he flips 10 fair coins?

> **Walk-Through**
>
> 1. Use complementary probability.
>
> 2. Let p be the probability that he gets more heads. Then, this must be the same probability that he gets more tails, thanks to symmetry. Hence, let q be the probability that he gets the same number of heads as that of tails.
>
> 3. There are five heads and tails to be selected for q. Compute q.
>
> 4. Subtract q from 1, and divide it by 2 to conclude solving the problem.

25. There are three math teams in the Bay area, with 5, 7, and 8 students respectively. Each team has two co-captains. If Bob randomly selects a team, and two members of that team to give a copy of "The Essential Guide to Competition Math," what is the probability that both of the people who receive books are co-captains?

> **Walk-Through**
>
> 1. Remember that $P(A \cap B) = P(A) \times P(B|A) = P(B) \times P(A|B)$, for two events A and B.
>
> 2. Find the probability of choosing the first team, then choosing two co-captains inside the first team.
>
> 3. Find the probability of choosing the second team, then choosing two co-captains inside the second team.
>
> 4. Find the probability of choosing the third team, then choosing two co-captains inside the third team.
>
> 5. Add the numbers found in step 2, 3, and 4, to conclude solving the problem.

26. What is the probability that $\overline{25d4}$ is divisible by 3, for any digit d?

> **Walk-Through**
>
> 1. Divisibility by 3 indicates that the sum of the digits is divisible by 3.
>
> 2. Count the total number of possible digits that can be placed inside d.
>
> 3. Count the number of d value(s) making $\overline{25d4}$ divisible by 3.
>
> 4. Divide step 3 by step 2 to conclude solving the problem.

TOPIC 3 Ending with Combinatorics

27. If any pair of two diagonals of a regular decagon is chosen, what is the probability that their intersection lies inside the decagon?

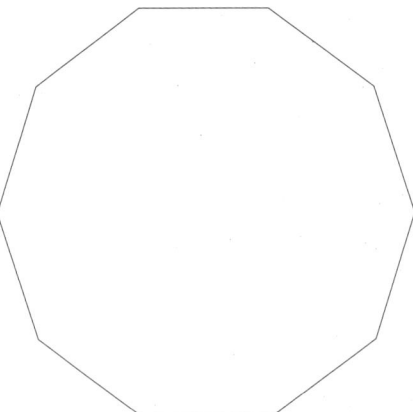

Walk-Through

1. Count the total number of diagonals formed inside the regular decagon.

2. Think about one-to-one correspondence between a pair of diagonals whose intersection point staying inside the decagon and a four-point quadrilateral whose vertices are chosen from those of regular decagon.

3. Divide the number found in step 2 by step 1 to conclude solving the problem.

28. If two different 2-digit positive integers are randomly chosen and multiplied together, what is the probability that the resulting product is even?

> **Walk-Through**
>
> 1. Count the number of 2-digit positive integers.
>
> 2. In order for the product to be even, the integers must be both non-odds.
>
> 3. Use complementary probability.
>
> 4. Let q be the probability of choosing two different odds.
>
> 5. Subtract q from 1 to conclude solving the problem.

29. A Math Circle has 20 members with 10 sophomores and 10 juniors. If a 4-person committee is chosen at random, what is the probability that the committee has at least 1 sophomore and at least 1 junior?

> **Walk-Through**
>
> 1. Use complementary probability.
>
> 2. Find the probability that the committee consists of all sophomores.
>
> 3. Find the probability that the committee consists of all juniors.
>
> 4. Add the probabilities found in step 2 and 3, and call it q.
>
> 5. Subtract q from 1 and conclude solving the problem.

30. A regular dodecahedron is a convex polyhedron with 12 regular pentagonal faces and 20 vertices. If two distinct vertices are chosen at random, what is the probability that the line connecting them does not lie inside the dodecahedron?

Walk-Through

1. Use complementary probability.

2. Use the Euler's formula $v - e + f = 2$ for dodecahedron.

3. Find the probability that the line contains edges.

4. Find the probability that the line contains the diagonals of any face.

5. Let q be the sum of probabilities in step 3 and 4.

6. Subtract q from 1 and conclude solving the problem.

31. Given a standard deck of 52 cards, with 4 cards in each of 13 ranks, if p is the probability that five cards chosen at random form a full house with 3 cards of one rank and 2 cards of another rank, such as $AA222$, $333QQ$, where $p = \dfrac{m}{n}$ where m and n are relatively prime, find the value of m.

> **Walk-Through**
>
> 1. Use constructive probability.
>
> 2. Let $\boxed{A}\,\boxed{A}\,\boxed{A}\,\boxed{B}\,\boxed{B}$ be one specific card selection.
>
> 3. Choose the rank that goes in A.
>
> 4. Choose the rank that goes in B.
>
> 5. Think about whether there is any overcount between step 3 and 4. Continue to step 6.
>
> 6. Compute the specific probability for $\boxed{A}\,\boxed{A}\,\boxed{A}\,\boxed{B}\,\boxed{B}$, in the written order.
>
> 7. Arrange $\boxed{A}\,\boxed{A}\,\boxed{A}\,\boxed{B}\,\boxed{B}$ in any order, and conclude solving the problem.

32. Given a rectangle of size 2021 by 2 with 4042 unit squares, the middle rectangle of 1 by 2 size is blotted out. If any rectangle from the figure is chosen at random, what is the probability that the rectangle does not include any part of the blotted-out rectangle?

> **Walk-Through**
>
> 1. Use complementary probability.
>
> 2. Choose a rectangle from the tiles above the blotted-out rectangle.
>
> 3. Choose a rectangle from the tiles below the blotted-out rectangle.
>
> 4. Find the total number of rectangles formed by choosing two vertical lines and two horizontal lines, containing edges shown in the figure.
>
> 5. Add the counts in step 2 and 3, and divide it by the count in step 4. Conclude solving the problem.

33. Bob has 6 children. Assuming that the gender of each child is determined independently and with equal likelihood of being male or female, what is the probability that Mr. Jones (whose first name must be Bob) has more sons than daughters or more daughters than sons?

Walk-Through

1. Use complementary probability.

2. Find the probability that the number of sons equals the number of daughters.

3. Let it be $\boxed{S}\boxed{S}\boxed{S}\boxed{D}\boxed{D}\boxed{D}$.

4. Find the specific probability laid out in step 3.

5. Arrange $\boxed{S}\boxed{S}\boxed{S}\boxed{D}\boxed{D}\boxed{D}$, since they are of different kinds.

6. Let the probability found in step 5 be q. Subtract q from 1, and conclude solving the problem.

34. Three cards are chosen at random from a standard 52-card deck. What is the probability that they are not all the same color?

> **Walk-Through**
>
> 1. Use complementary probability.
>
> 2. Find the probability that all three cards are red.
>
> 3. Find the probability that all three cards are black.
>
> 4. Add the probabilities in step 2 and 3, and call it as q.
>
> 5. Subtract q from 1, and conclude solving the problem.

35. If eight points are equally spaced on a unit circle, what is the probability that a triangle formed by connecting three out of eight points is obtuse?

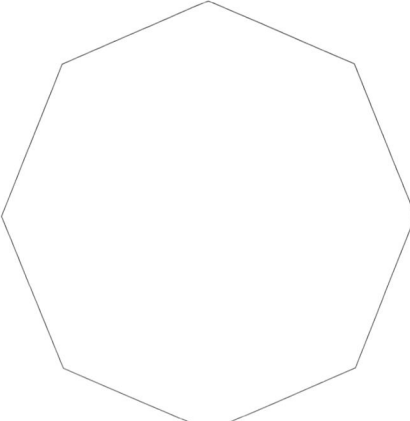

> **Walk-Through**
>
> 1. Count obtuse triangles having two edges of a regular octagon as their sides.
>
> 2. Count obtuse triangles having one edge of a regular octagon as their side.
>
> 3. Add the number of triangles in step 1 and 2.
>
> 4. Divide by the total number of triangles formed by connecting three vertices of a regular octagon.

Answer Key

1. $\dfrac{8}{15}$

In order for the product of the values is even, we only need to eliminate the possibility when the product is odd. This happens when the face values are $1, 3$, or 5. Hence, the probability that the product of the values is even is $\dfrac{15}{16}$. Out of these probabilities, the sum is odd if and only if we have 3 evens with 1 odd or 1 even with 3 odds. Hence, there are four possible cases. In other words, the answer is $\dfrac{8/16}{15/16} = \dfrac{8}{15}$.

2. $\dfrac{1}{4}$

If $a = -2$, then $b = 2$. If $a = 0$, then $b = 2, 3, 4, \cdots, 7$. If $a = 2$, then $b = 2$. If $a = 3$, then $b = 3$. If $a = 4$, then $b = 2, 4$. If $a = 5$, then $b = 5$. Hence, the probability we want is $\dfrac{12}{8 \cdot 6} = \dfrac{1}{4}$.

3. $\dfrac{1}{663}$

There are four possible cases. In this solution, we call an ace as 1.
First, $(3\diamond, 1\diamond, 1*) = \dfrac{3}{52 \cdot 51 \cdot 50}$.
Second, $(3\diamond, X\diamond, 1*) = \dfrac{1 \cdot 11 \cdot 4}{52 \cdot 51 \cdot 50}$.
Third, $(3*, 1\diamond, 1*) = \dfrac{3 \cdot 1 \cdot 3}{52 \cdot 51 \cdot 50}$.
Fourth, $(3*, X\diamond, 1*) = \dfrac{3 \cdot 12 \cdot 4}{52 \cdot 51 \cdot 50}$.
Hence, the sum of all these values is $\dfrac{1}{663}$.

4. $\dfrac{9}{32}$

Draw a tree diagram to find out that we get $RRRR$ if we choose RBB, BRB, and BBR. Hence, the probability we want is $\dfrac{1}{16} + \dfrac{3}{32} + \dfrac{1}{8} = \dfrac{9}{32}$.

5. $\dfrac{88}{169}$

Without a diamond nor king, there are 36 cards left. Since we allow replacement, the probability must be $1 - (\dfrac{36}{52})^2 = \dfrac{88}{169}$.

6. $\dfrac{319}{324}$

We use complementary probability. Compute the probability of having no two dice sharing equal numerical value, i.e., $\dfrac{6!}{6^6} = \dfrac{5}{324}$. Hence, the probability must be $\dfrac{319}{324}$.

7. $\dfrac{7775}{7776}$

If at most four of the five dice show a 6, we must eliminate the case when there are five 6's. Hence, the probability must be $1 - \dfrac{1}{6^5} = \dfrac{7775}{7776}$.

8. $\dfrac{3}{16}$

Try out a few trials. You can tell that Bob should go up for the first two times. Then, there are six possibilities from then on. Hence, the probability must be $\dfrac{6}{32} = \dfrac{3}{16}$.

9. $\dfrac{29}{36}$

Get rid of all non-composite numbers. $1 = 1 \cdot 1$, $2 = 1 \cdot 2, 2 \cdot 1$, and $3 = 1 \cdot 3, 3 \cdot 1$, and $5 = 1 \cdot 5, 5 \cdot 1$. Therefore, we get $1 - \dfrac{7}{36} = \dfrac{29}{36}$.

10. $\dfrac{73}{100}$

Think about complements. Let $ab \leq 10$. If $ab = 10$, there are 4 possible pairs. If $ab = 9$, there are 3 possible pairs. If $ab = 8$, there are 4 pairs. If $ab = 7$, there are 2 pairs. If $ab = 6$, there are 4 pairs. If $ab = 5$, there are 2 pairs. If $ab = 4$, there are 3 pairs. If $ab = 3$, there are 2 pairs. If $ab = 2$, there are 2 pairs. If $ab = 1$, there is 1 pair. Hence, there are 27 pairs to exclude. Therefore, the probability of $ab > 10$ is $\dfrac{73}{100}$.

11. $\dfrac{13}{18}$

Finding it directly, we may compute two odds and two evens, i.e, $\dfrac{25}{36}$ and $\dfrac{1}{36}$. Therefore, the sum must be $\dfrac{26}{36} = \dfrac{13}{18}$.

12. $\dfrac{91}{216}$

We may come up with three possibilities. The probability of winning is $\dfrac{1}{6}$ and the probability of losing is $\dfrac{5}{6}$. Hence, we get $\dfrac{1}{6}, \dfrac{5}{6} \cdot \dfrac{1}{6}$, and $\dfrac{5}{6} \cdot \dfrac{5}{6} \cdot \dfrac{1}{6}$. Hence, the probability of winning before the fourth turn is $\dfrac{91}{216}$.

13. $\dfrac{25}{28}$

We only eliminate the probability of having 35 dollars. Hence, we only get $(25, 5, 5)$, $(5, 25, 5)$ or $(5, 5, 25)$. Hence, $\dfrac{3}{9} \cdot \dfrac{3}{8} \cdot \dfrac{2}{7} \cdot 3 = \dfrac{3}{28}$. Thus, the answer must be $\dfrac{25}{28}$.

14. $\dfrac{72}{425}$

$$\dfrac{13 \cdot 12 \cdot \binom{4}{2} \cdot \binom{4}{1}}{\binom{52}{3}} = \dfrac{72}{425}$$

15. $\dfrac{1}{8}$

Since $70^{11} = 2^{11} 5^{11} 7^{11}$, we can find $12 \cdot 12 \cdot 12$ number of positive factors. Since there are $\dfrac{70^{11}}{70^6} = 70^5$ number of multiples, we may find $6 \cdot 6 \cdot 6$ number of positive factors of $7^5 2^5 5^5$. Therefore, the answer is $\dfrac{6 \cdot 6 \cdot 6}{12 \cdot 12 \cdot 12} = \dfrac{1}{8}$.

16. $\dfrac{1}{24}$

We only allow $(1, 1, P)$, $(1, P, 1)$ and $(P, 1, 1)$. Hence, the answer must be $\dfrac{1}{6} \cdot \dfrac{1}{6} \cdot \dfrac{3}{6} \cdot 3 = \dfrac{1}{24}$.

17. $\dfrac{89}{245}$

$$ab + a + b \equiv -1 \pmod{5}$$
$$ab + a + b + 1 \equiv 0 \pmod{5}$$
$$(a+1)(b+1) \equiv 0 \pmod{5}$$

Hence, $a + 1$ is a multiple of 5 or $b + 1$ is a multiple of 5. Thus,

$$\dfrac{10 \cdot 49 + 49 \cdot 10 - 10 \cdot 9}{50 \cdot 49} = \dfrac{89}{245}$$

18. 144

p can be computed as

$$10 \times 9 \times \dfrac{4}{40} \times \dfrac{3}{39} \times \dfrac{2}{38} \times \dfrac{4}{37} \times 4 = \dfrac{144}{9139}$$

the answer must be 144.

19. $\dfrac{25}{36}$

Case 1. $aabbc$: $\dfrac{\binom{6}{2} \cdot 4}{6^5} \cdot \dfrac{5!}{2!2!}$

Case 2. $aabcd$: $\dfrac{6 \cdot \binom{5}{3}}{6^5} \cdot \dfrac{5!}{2!}$

Hence, add them up to get $\dfrac{25}{36}$.

20. $\dfrac{3}{14}$

Out of all possible cases $8!$, we get $12 \times 6!$. Hence, the probability we want is
$$\dfrac{12 \cdot 6!}{8!} = \dfrac{3}{14}.$$

21. $\dfrac{421}{1296}$

We must perform caseworks to get
$$(\dfrac{2}{3})^4 + \dfrac{1}{6} \cdot \dfrac{1}{6} \cdot (\dfrac{2}{3})^2 \cdot \dfrac{4!}{2!} + (\dfrac{1}{6})^4 \cdot \dfrac{4!}{2!2!}$$

Get rid of these cases from 1 and divide it by 2 to get $\dfrac{421}{1296}$.

22. 69

Find the value of p as
$$\dfrac{\binom{10}{2} \cdot 4 \cdot 3 \cdot 4 \cdot 3}{40 \cdot 39 \cdot 38 \cdot 37} \times \dfrac{4!}{2!2!}$$

Simplifying it as much as possible, we get $\dfrac{a \cdot b \cdot c}{13 \cdot 19 \cdot 37}$. Hence, $p + q + r = 69$.

23. $\dfrac{24}{35}$

Set up $aabc$, so that we get
$$\binom{4}{1} \times \binom{3}{2} \times \dfrac{2 \cdot 1 \cdot 2 \cdot 2}{8 \cdot 7 \cdot 6 \cdot 5} \times \dfrac{4!}{2!}$$

Hence, we get $\dfrac{24}{35}$.

24. $\dfrac{193}{512}$

$1 - \dfrac{\binom{10}{5}}{2^{10}} = 2p$ where p is the probability of having more heads than tails. Hence, $p = \dfrac{193}{512}$.

25. $\dfrac{11}{180}$

$$\dfrac{1}{3} \times \dfrac{\binom{2}{2}}{\binom{5}{2}} + \dfrac{1}{3} \times \dfrac{\binom{2}{2}}{\binom{7}{2}} + \dfrac{1}{3} \times \dfrac{\binom{2}{2}}{\binom{8}{2}} = \dfrac{11}{180}$$

26. $\dfrac{3}{10}$

Since $\overline{25d4}$ is divisible by 3 if and only if $2 + 5 + d + 4$ is a multiple of 3, we get $d = 1, 4, 7$. Hence, there are 10 possible digits we can use for d, so the answer must be $\dfrac{3}{10}$.

27. $\dfrac{6}{17}$

There are $\dfrac{10 \cdot 7}{2} = 35$ number of diagonals in regular decagon. Hence, we get the total number of intersection point as $\binom{35}{2}$. However, the intersection point lies inside the decagon if and only if the two diagonals form a quadrilateral. Therefore, the number of intersection points that lie inside the decagon is exactly same as the number of quadrilaterals formed out of 10 points. Hence, we get $\binom{10}{4}$ number of intersection points within the decagon. Thus, the answer must be $\binom{10}{4}/\binom{35}{2} = 6/17$.

28. $\dfrac{67}{89}$

We substract the number of cases when the product is odd. Hence, $1 - \dfrac{\binom{45}{2}}{\binom{90}{2}} = \dfrac{67}{89}$.

29. $\dfrac{295}{323}$

We substract the probabilities when the committee members are formed out of either sophomores or juniors, i.e., $1 - \dfrac{2\binom{10}{4}}{\binom{20}{4}} = \dfrac{295}{323}$.

30. $\dfrac{9}{19}$

Using Euler's formula, $v + f = e + 2$, we get the number of edges as 30. Also, out of one pentagonal face, there are 5 diagonals formed. Therefore, there are 60 diagonals on the faces in total and 30 edges in total. Hence, the line connecting the vertices of dodecahedron do not lie inside the figure with the probability of $\dfrac{60 + 30}{190} = \dfrac{9}{19}$.

31. 6

The probability we want for $aaabb$ can be given by

$$13 \times 12 \times \dfrac{4 \cdot 3 \cdot 2 \cdot 4 \cdot 3}{52 \cdot 51 \cdot 50 \cdot 49 \cdot 48} \times \dfrac{5!}{3!2!} = \dfrac{6}{4165}$$

Hence, $m = 6$.

32. $\dfrac{1010}{2021}$

$$\dfrac{2\binom{3}{2}\binom{1011}{2}}{\binom{3}{2}\binom{2022}{2}} = \dfrac{1010}{2021}$$

33. $\dfrac{11}{16}$

$$1 - \dfrac{\binom{6}{3}}{2^6} = \dfrac{11}{16}$$

34. $\dfrac{13}{17}$

$$1 - \dfrac{2 \cdot \binom{26}{3}}{\binom{52}{3}} = \dfrac{13}{17}$$

35. $\dfrac{3}{7}$

Fix an edge. There are 2 obtuse triangles using adjacent edges. Also, there are 2 obtuse triangles using non-adjacent edges. Since the first 2 obtuse triangles are overcounted, we need to divide by 2. Now, we let our fixed edge free and count how many edges we have. We have 8 edges, so there are 8 obtuse triangles formed using two adjacent edges and 16 obtuse triangles formed using one edge. Thus,

$$\dfrac{8 + 16}{\binom{8}{3}} = \dfrac{24}{56} = \dfrac{3}{7}$$

TOPIC 4

Beginning with Number Theory

4.1 Divisors and Remainders

4.2 Parity and Modular Arithmetic

4.3 Practices

4.1 Divisors and Remainders

This section deals with Number Theory. We would like to see the meaning of divisors. Let n and d be integers satisfying $n \geq d$. Then,

$$n = dk$$

where k is an integer. In this case, we say d is a divisor of n, or n is a multiple of d. This naturally brings forth the topic of prime factorization. Primes are positive integers greater than 1 such that there are only two positive divisors, i.e., 1 and itself.

- 2 : the only even prime.
- 3 : the smallest odd prime.
- $6k \pm 1$: other odd primes.

Each integer has a unique prime factorization, and we use it to find the number of divisors or the sum of divisors. Let $n = p_1^{e_1} p_2^{e_2} \cdots p_k^{e_k}$. Then,

- Number of divisors : $(e_1 + 1)(e_2 + 1)(e_3 + 1) \cdots (e_k + 1)$
- Sum of divisors :
  $(1 + p_1 + p_1^2 + \cdots + p_1^{e_1})(1 + p_2 + p_2^2 + \cdots + p_2^{e_2}) \cdots (1 + p_k + p_k^2 + \cdots + p_k^{e_k})$

Due to prime factorization, we may compare two integers by finding the greatest common divisor and the least common multiple. Let $a = p_1^{e_1} p_2^{e_2} \cdots p_n^{e_n}$, and $b = q_1^{f_1} q_2^{f_2} \cdots q_m^{e_m}$. Then,

- $\gcd(a, b)$=common prime factors$^{\text{minimum (common) exponents of the two}}$
- $\text{lcm}(a, b) = \dfrac{ab}{\gcd(a, b)}$

Let's have a look at the following example.

Example Given two integers $12, 18$, find both $\gcd(12, 18)$ and $\text{lcm}(12, 18)$.

Solution First off, $12 = 2^2 3^1$ and $18 = 2^1 3^2$. Then, $\gcd(12, 18)$ equals $2^1 3^1$. Also, $\text{lcm}(12, 18)$ equals $2^2 3^2$ because $\dfrac{12 \cdot 18}{2^1 3^1} = \dfrac{2^3 3^3}{2^1 3^1} = 2^2 3^2$. Instead of using the formula we may say that the least common multiple is
(any prime factor that appears)$^{\text{maximum exponent of the two}}$. However, it is common for us to use the following equation, assuming that a and b are both positive integers,

$$a \times b = \gcd(a, b) \times \text{lcm}(a, b)$$

On the other hand, if $n \neq dk$, then we may come up with the long division form such that

$$n = dk + r$$

where $0 \leq r < d$. This leads to two different applications, i.e., Euclidean Algorithm using the Well-Ordering Principle or modular arithmetic system that simplifies integer equations. In this book, we would like to focus more on modular arithmetic system so that we may be able to solve a system of modular equations using Chinese Remainder Theorem, which is frequently asked in competition math.

That being said, I cannot move on without mentioning Euclidean algorithm. Instead of showing the generic form of the algorithm, I present you with the example so that we can follow the form easily in the test.

Example Find the greatest common divisor between 234 and 112.

Solution Notice that 112 is smaller than 234. Divide 234 by 112. Then, the remainder must be $10 = 234 - 2(112)$. Now, perform another division of 112 by 10. The remainder must be $2 = 112 - 10(11)$. Perform another division of 10 by 2. The remainder is $0 = 10 - 2(5)$. Then, we stop there. We say that the remainder is 2. If we use the greatest common divisor of a and b as (a, b), we may write this process as $(234, \mathbf{112}) = (112, \mathbf{10}) = (10, \mathbf{2}) = (2, \mathbf{0})$.

As we keep performing long division, we can easily see that the remainders are somehow approaching 0. It is easy to see why that happens because we keep dividing out or subtracting the numbers away. However, how do we guarantee that this process eventually stops? This is because we used the Well-Ordering Principle, which is a special property of the set of whole numbers. We will not prove it in this book, but this sounds quite natural to us. Suppose I give you a finite set of whole numbers $N = \{a_1, a_2, a_3, \cdots, a_k\}$. Even though this may not be rearranged in a proper order from least to greatest, we may find the smallest element in the set. Call it a_m. Then, $N = \{a_m, a_1, \cdots, a_k\}$ where $a_m \leq a_1 \leq \cdots a_k$. The Well-Ordering Principle guarantees that we have the smallest element in the set of whole numbers.

Why does this matter? Have a look at our example. Since $a = dk + r$ where $0 \leq r < d$, and $10 \to 2 \to 0$, we keep going down towards 0, and when we eventually hit 0, we stop. We know for sure that we will hit 0 due to the Well-Ordering Principle.

4.2 Parity and Modular Arithmetic

What is the application of long division, other than Euclidean Algorithm? I usually refer this phenomenon as "changing the lens." The easiest and most common example is parity (evenness and oddness).

Even integers can be written as $n = 2k$ while odd integers can be written as $n = 2k + 1$. What is the significance of this method? It is quite useful for us to see the world of integers into binary modes, either even or odd, because it simplifies the problem into a simpler one. However, this may simplify a complex problem way too simple, so we may be careful of which lens we use. What could be better than lens of multiples of 2? It will be multiples of 4. In other words, we can categorize all integers into four types : $4k$, $4k + 1$, $4k + 2$, and $4k + 3$. Even integers can be written as either $4k$ or $4k + 2$, or odd integers may be written as either $4k + 1$ or $4k + 3$. Choosing a higher number multiple will lead us to specific categorization of numbers.

Sometimes, this may be useful to figure out the properties of perfect squares.

- $n = 4k : n^2 = 16k = 4(4k)$, divisible by 4.

- $n = 4k + 1 : n^2 = (4k+1)^2 = 16k^2 + 8k + 1 = 4(4k^2 + 2k) + 1$, **not divisible by** 4.

- $n = 4k + 2 : n^2 = (4k+2)^2 = 16k^2 + 16k + 4 = 4(4k^2 + 4k + 1)$, **divisible by** 4.

- $n = 4k + 3 : n^2 = (4k+3)^2 = 16k^2 + 24k + 9 = 4(4k^2 + 6k + 2) + 1$, **not divisible by** 4.

Interesting feature we figured out in the previous categorization is that n^2 will always have the remainder of 0 or 1 when divided by 4.

Is there a simpler way to write the above property? The answer to this question requires modular arithmetic. If a is a multiple of n, then we say

$$a \equiv 0 \pmod{n}$$

which can be written as a is equivalent to 0 mod n. In the previous example, we may say that $n^2 \equiv 0 \pmod 4$ or $n^2 \equiv 1 \pmod 4$. This modular arithmetic system is extremely useful because we may substitute a number by a simpler number. Have a look at the following example.

Example Solve $7n \equiv -1 \pmod{20}$.

Solution First off, what is the meaning of $-1 \pmod{20}$? It refers to the set of numbers $\{\cdots, -21, -1, 19, 39, 59, \cdots\}$. Out of these numbers, we are looking for multiples of 7. Hence, $7n \equiv -1 \equiv -21 \pmod{20}$, so $n \equiv -3 \equiv 17 \pmod{20}$.

4.3 Practices

1. How many different counting numbers will each leave a remainder of 6 when divided into 48?

Walk-Through

1. Paraphrase "a remainder of 6 when divided into 48" using letters.

2. For example, $48 = nq + 6$ where $n > 6$.

3. $42 = nq$ for integer values of n and q.

4. Solve for n.

2. If p, q, and r are prime numbers, find the number of (p, q, r) satisfying $p - q - 8$ and $q - r - 8$ are both prime.

> **Walk-Through**
>
> 1. Notice that primes are either 2, 3 or $6k \pm 1$ for some k.
>
> 2. Begin with $q - r - 8$ being a prime. Try caseworking with $q - r - 8$ as 2, 3 or $6k \pm 1$.
>
> 3. Reason why q can't be either 2 or 3.
>
> 4. Assume $q = 6k + 1$. Find one value of k that makes sense, satisfying all given conditions.
>
> 5. Assume $q = 6k - 1$. Reason why this leads to contradiction.
>
> 6. Find all values of p, and conclude solving the problem.

3. If $4 \leq n \leq 12$, find the sum of all n's such that the remainder of when n^2 is divided by 12 equals the remainder when n is divided by 12.

Walk-Through

1. The remainder when n^2 is divided by 12 can be written as n^2 (mod 12).

2. Likewise, the remainder when n is divided by 12 can be written as n (mod 12).

3. Solve for $n^2 \equiv n$ (mod 12).

4. $n(n-1) \equiv 0$ (mod 12), so check it with $n = 4, 5, 6, 7, \cdots, 12$.

TOPIC 3 Ending with Combinatorics

4. Given a sequence $A = \{130, 127, 124, \cdots, 13\}$ and $B = \{3, 7, 11, \cdots, 139\}$, find the number of terms that are common to both sequence A and B.

> **Walk-Through**
>
> 1. Rewrite a term in the sequence A as $x \equiv 13 \pmod{3}$. Reason why it works.
>
> 2. Rewrite a term in the sequence B as $x \equiv 3 \pmod{4}$. Reason why it works.
>
> 3. Find the first few terms in the first equation and the second equation.
>
> 4. Find the smallest positive common number in the equations.
>
> 5. $x \equiv$ "common number" $\pmod{\text{lcm}(3,4)}$. Now, rewrite it in terms of non-modular equation.
>
> 6. Set up an inequality that x is between 13 and 130.

5. If the current time is exact midnight, what time in hours and minutes will it be in 1234 minutes?

> **Walk-Through**
>
> 1. Rewrite it in terms of modular equation.
>
> 2. Rewrite it in terms of long-division form.
>
> 3. Notice that modular equation is fit for classification. In other words, if the problem searches for minutes, then modular equation is a perfect fit.
>
> 4. Notice that long-division form is fit for specific solution or counting with inequality. Since the problem searches for specific hours and minutes, this form is a better fit.

6. What is the remainder when 2^{2020} is divided by 13?

> **Walk-Through**
>
> 1. According to Fermat's Little Theorem, $a^{p-1} \equiv 1 \pmod{p}$ where p is a prime number and a is relatively prime to p.
>
> 2. Without applying FLT to the problem, find the patterns of remainder by iterating powers of 2 in mod 13.
>
> 3. Or, one can further use $2^6 = 64 \equiv -1 \pmod{13}$ with the binomial theorem, i.e., $(a+b)^n = \binom{n}{0}a^n b^0 + \binom{n}{1}a^{n-1}b^1 + \cdots + \binom{n}{n}a^0 b^n$.

7. Out of 4-digit numbers with last two zeroes, the number is special if it has a remainder of 200 or 600 when divided by 900. How many special numbers are there between 1999 and 4099?

Walk-Through

1. A number that has a remainder of 200 when divided by 900 can be written as $n = 900q + 200$ for some q.

2. Likewise, a number that has a remainder of 600 when divided by 900 can be written as $n = 900q' + 600$ for some q'.

3. Set up inequality for q and q'.

4. Find the values of q and q' satisfying the given inequalities.

8. For how many integer values of n between 1 and 100 inclusive does the decimal representation of $\dfrac{n}{140}$ terminate?

Walk-Through

1. Prime factorize 140.

2. If the denominator has 7 in its prime factorization form, $\dfrac{n}{140}$ does not terminate.

3. Hence, n should be a multiple of 7 between 1 and 100.

4. Find all multiples of 7 between 1 and 100 by setting up an inequality.

9. A *relatively prime* date is a date for which the number of the month and the number of the day are relatively prime. How many relatively prime dates are in June?

> **Walk-Through**
>
> 1. Prime factorize 30.
>
> 2. Take out positive multiples of 2 smaller than or equal to 30.
>
> 3. Take out positive multiples of 3 smaller than or equal to 30.
>
> 4. Add positive multiples of 6 smaller than or equal to 30, thanks to the principle of inclusion and exclusion.

10. A positive integer is 3 more than a multiple of 4 and 4 more than a multiple of 5. What is the second least integer?

Walk-Through

1. Let a positive integer be n.

2. Then, rewrite 3 more than a multiple of 4 into $n \equiv 3 \pmod{4}$.

3. Likewise, rewrite 4 more than a multiple of 5 into $n \equiv 4 \pmod{5}$.

4. Solve for the system of modular equations either by Chinese Remainder Theorem or by finding the smallest common number in each equation.

5. Find the second least integer and conclude solving the problem.

11. Find the sum of all positive integer values of n for which $\dfrac{n+24}{n}$ is an integer.

Walk-Through

1. Turn $\dfrac{n+24}{n}$ into $1 + \dfrac{24}{n}$.

2. In order for $\dfrac{24}{n}$ to be an integer, n must be a divisor of 24.

3. Prime factorize 24.

4. Find the sum of all divisors of 24 by using the prime factorization form of 24.

12. How many fractions in the form $\frac{n}{99}$ for positive integer n smaller than 99 are in lowest terms?

> **Walk-Through**
>
> 1. A fraction in the lowest term means that it has been already factorized.
>
> 2. The values of n can't be multiples of 3 nor 11.
>
> 3. Use the principle of inclusion and exclusion to find the values of n satisfying the given condition.
>
> 4. Or, one may use Euler's phi($=\phi$) formula to solve for this. In other words, $\phi(99)$ produces the same answer.
>
> 5. For relatively prime a and b, $\phi(ab) = \phi(a)\phi(b)$, where $\phi(n)$ is the number of positive integers smaller than or equal to n such that they are relatively prime to n. Try finding $\phi(99)$ by finding $\phi(9)$ and $\phi(11)$.

13. Bob writes down a and b, a perfect square and a cube that are the smallest positive multiples of 20, respectively. What is the difference between b and a?

> **Walk-Through**
>
> 1. a is a perfect square and a multiple of 20. So, let $a = 20k$. Now, rewrite k in terms of different letters to make $20k$ as a perfect square.
>
> 2. b is a perfect cube and a multiple of 20. So, let $a = 20k'$. Now, rewrite k' in terms of different letters to make $20k'$ as a perfect cube.
>
> 3. Conclude solving the problem by finding the difference between b and a.

TOPIC 3 Ending with Combinatorics

14. For how many natural numbers less than or equal to 100 have the sum of prime factors equal to 5, where there are more than one prime factor? (In other words, a number of form 5^k is not under consideration.)

Walk-Through

1. Let n be a natural number smaller than or equal to 100.

2. Let $n = 2^x \cdot 3^y$ where $x \geq 1$ and $y \geq 1$, according to the condition laid out in the problem.

3. Perform casework on the values of x. Find all respective values of y for each x.

15. If a positive integer n is multiplied to $1^1 2^2 3^3 4^4 5^5 6^6 7^7 8^8 9^9$, it becomes a perfect square. Find the smallest possible value of n.

> **Walk-Through**
>
> 1. Notice that expressions with even exponents are already perfect squares.
>
> 2. Check with power expressions with odd powers.
>
> 3. Multiply the smallest possible value of integers that will turn odd powers into even powers.
>
> 4. One do not need to prime factorize the given expression to solve for n.

TOPIC 3 Ending with Combinatorics 145

16. If a number ends in zeros, the zeros are called terminal zeros. For instance, 1000 has three terminal zeros and 543210 has one terminal zero. If $N = 20!$, how many terminal zeros does N have?

> **Walk-Through**
>
> 1. Find the powers of 2 for a prime factorization form of 20!, which is also known as 2-adic number of 20!.
>
> 2. Find the powers of 5 for a prime factorization form of 20!, which is known as 5-adic number of 20!.
>
> 3. Choose the smaller of the two, and conclude solving the problem.

17. The number 1000! has a long tail of terminal zeros. How many terminal zeros are there?

> **Walk-Through**
>
> 1. Find the powers of 2 for a prime factorization form of 1000!, which is also known as 2-adic number of 1000!.
>
> 2. Find the powers of 5 for a prime factorization form of 1000!, which is known as 5-adic number of 1000!.
>
> 3. Choose the smaller of the two, and conclude solving the problem.

18. Find the product of the exponents of the prime factorization of the largest perfect square that divides $12! = 12 \times 11 \times 10 \times \cdots \times 1$. (For example, if 36 is the largest perfect square that divides a certain given number, the product of the exponents of the prime factorization of 36 is 4.)

Walk-Through

1. Use the method applied in the previous two problems to find out the exponents of 2, 3, 5, 7 and 11.

2. Compute the largest possible perfect square that divides 12! by looking at the unique prime factorization of 12!.

3. Compute the product of the exponents of the prime factorization of the largest perfect square found in step 2.

19. Find the remainder when $9 \times 99 \times 999 \times \cdots \times 999999$ is divided by 100.

Walk-Through

1. Evaluate each number in mod 100.

2. Compute the modular expression in mod 100.

3. If the resulting number shows up in negative value, turn it into positive number by adding multiples of 100. Make sure that the remainder is at least 0 but at most 99, inclusive.

20. Out of all positive divisors of $2^{12} - 1$, how many divisors are divisible by 3?

Walk-Through

1. Use $a^2 - b^2 = (a-b)(a+b)$.

2. Use $a^3 - b^3 = (a-b)(a^2 + ab + b^2)$.

3. Use $a^3 + b^3 = (a+b)(a^2 - ab + b^2)$.

4. Find the number of expressions with 3^n-free factors.

5. Find the number of expressions for 3^n-factors.

6. Multiply the numbers found in step 4 and 5.

Answer Key

1. 4

$48 \equiv 6 \pmod{n}$ implies that $42 \equiv 0 \pmod{n}$. This implies that n must be a divisor of 42. We can directly find and count count all the divisors of 42, i.e., $1, 2, 3, 6, 7, 14, 21$, and 42.

Since the remainder cannot be greater than n, we get $n = 7, 14, 21$, and 42. There are 4 values of n.

2. 2

It is obvious that we start from $q - r - 8$ being a prime. Hence, $q - r - 8 = 2, 3, 6k \pm 1$ for some positive integer k. Other than 2, $q - r - 8$ must be odd. Hence, $q - r$ must be odd as well. In this case, $r = 2$, and $q = 13$. This $q = 13$ is the only possible prime we can get. If $q = 6k + 1$ for some other k's, then $q - 2 - 8 = 6k + 1 - 10 = 6k - 9 = 3(2k - 3)$ is no longer prime for $k > 1$. If $q = 6k - 1$, then $6k - 1 - 2 - 8 = 6k - 11$, which can be prime itself but gets a contradictory result when we see the first condition $p - q - 8$ being a prime. In other words, $p - (6k - 1) - 8 = p - (6k - 9)$ should be prime. Now, it is obvious that p cannot be 2 nor 3. So, we must think about $p \equiv \pm 1 \pmod{6}$. This implies that $p - (6k - 9) \equiv \pm 1 \pmod{6}$ is indeed contradictory. Hence, q cannot be $6k - 1$-form prime. Therefore, $q = 13$ is the only prime. Hence, $p - 13 - 8$ is a prime. p must be 23 because odd-odd-even must be even. If $q - r - 8$ is 2, then $13 - 3 - 8$ works as well.

Therefore, there are two possible triples (p, q, r), i.e. $(23, 13, 2), (23, 13, 3)$.

3. 25

Since $n^2 \equiv n \pmod{12}$, we get $n^2 - n \equiv 0 \pmod{12}$. Thus, $n(n - 1) \equiv 0 \pmod{12}$. By plugging all possible values of n into the quadratic modular equation, we get $n = 4, 9, 12$ as working solutions. The answer must be 25.

4. 10

Let x be the number on sequence A and B. Then, $x \equiv 13 \pmod{3}$ and $x \equiv 3 \pmod{4}$. Thus, $x \equiv 1 \pmod{3}$ implies that $x = 3k + 1$. Substitute the expression into the second one to get $3k + 1 \equiv 3 \pmod{4}$, i.e., $3k \equiv 2 \pmod{4}$. Thus, $k \equiv 2 \pmod{4}$. This implies that $k = 4p + 1$ for some integer p. Hence, $x = 3(4p + 1) + 1 = 12p + 4$. We start from $p = 1$ and end at $p = 10$. Thus, there are 10 terms common to both sequence A and B.

5. $8:34$ PM

$$1234 = 1200 + 34$$
$$\equiv 34 \pmod{60}$$

This being said, 1234 minutes must be equal to 20 hours and 34 minutes passed since the midnight. Hence, the time must be $8:34$ PM.

6. 3

By Fermat's Little Theorem, $2^{12} \equiv 1 \pmod{13}$. Divide 2020 by 12 to get the remainder of 4. Hence, $2^4 \equiv 16 \equiv 3 \pmod{13}$. The answer must be 3.

7. 5

Since $1999 < 900a + 200 < 4099$, we get $a = 2, 3, 4$. Likewise, since $1999 < 900b + 600 < 4099$, we get $b = 2, 3$. There are five values in total.

8. 14

In order to terminate $\frac{n}{140}$, we need to eliminate multiples of 7 since $140 = 2^2 \cdot 5 \cdot 7$. Hence, $\lfloor \frac{100}{7} \rfloor = 14$.

9. 10

First, $30 = 2 \cdot 3 \cdot 5$. Hence, out of 30 positive integers, we take out multiples of 2 or 3. Hence, $30 - \lfloor \frac{30}{2} \rfloor - \lfloor \frac{30}{3} \rfloor + \lfloor \frac{30}{6} \rfloor = 10$.

10. 39

First, $n \equiv 3 \pmod{4}$. Likewise, $n \equiv 4 \pmod{5}$. Hence, $4k + 3 \equiv 4 \pmod{5}$ implies that $4k \equiv 1 \pmod{5}$. Hence, $k \equiv -1 \pmod{5}$. Put $k = 5x + 4$ back into the $n = 4k + 3$ to get $n = 19, 39, \cdots$. The second smallest number in the list is 39. Or, you could try it this way. If $n \equiv 3 \pmod{4}$ and $n \equiv 4 \pmod{5}$, then $n + 1 \equiv 0 \pmod{4}$ & $\pmod{5}$, so $n + 1 = 20k$ for some integer k. Hence, $n + 1 = 20, 40, \cdots$, so $n_2 = 39$.

11. 60

Rearrange $\frac{n + 24}{n}$ into $1 + \frac{24}{n}$. Now, in order for this expression to be an integer, set $\frac{24}{n}$ as an integer. Hence, n must be a divisor of 24, i.e., $24 = 2^3 \cdot 3^1$. The sum of all positive integer divisors can be computed as $(1 + 2 + 2^2 + 2^3)(1 + 3) = 60$.

12. 60

We are looking for n smaller than 99 that is relatively prime to 99. There are 98 numbers in total, and 32 multiples of 3 and 8 multiples of 11, and 2 multiples of 33. Hence, $98 - 32 - 8 + 2 = 60$ is the answer.

13. 900

First, $20 = 2^2 \cdot 5$. Hence, $a = 100$ and $b = 2^3 \cdot 5^3 = 1000$. The difference between the two numbers is 900.

14. 9

According to the given information, such natural number must be in the form of $2^\alpha 3^\beta$. Hence, case-working on α, we get $2 \cdot 3, 2 \cdot 3^2, 2 \cdot 3^3, 2^2 \cdot 3^1, 2^2 \cdot 3^2, 2^3 \cdot 3, 2^3 \cdot 3^2, 2^4 \cdot 3, 2^5 \cdot 3$. There are 9 numbers satisfying the given property.

15. 105

Rewriting the given expression, we get $2^{40} \cdot 3^{27} \cdot 5^5 \cdot 7^7$. The smallest n should be $3 \cdot 5 \cdot 7 = 105$ so that the exponents are all even.

16. 4

First,
$\lfloor 20/2 \rfloor + \lfloor 20/4 \rfloor + \lfloor 20/8 \rfloor + \lfloor 20/16 \rfloor = 18$ implies that 2^{18} divides 20!. Likewise, $\lfloor 20/5 \rfloor = 4$ implies that 5^4 divides 20!. Hence, there are 4 terminal zeros N has. Refer to Legendre's Formula in the following page.

17. 249

$\lfloor 1000/5 \rfloor + \lfloor 1000/25 \rfloor + \lfloor 1000/125 \rfloor + \lfloor 1000/625 \rfloor = 249$. Just like in question # 16, refer to Legendre's Formula.

18. 80

$12! = 2^{10} \cdot 3^5 \cdot 5^2 \cdot 7 \cdot 11$ implies that $2^{10} \cdot 3^4 \cdot 5^2$ is the largest perfect square that divides 12!. Hence, the product of the exponents of this largest square is $10 \cdot 4 \cdot 2 = 80$.

19. 91

$$9 \cdot (100-1) \cdot (1000-1) \cdots$$
$$= 9 \cdot 99 \cdot 999$$
$$\equiv 9 \cdot -1 \cdot -1 \cdot -1 \cdots -1 \pmod{100}.$$

Hence, the answer must be $-9 \equiv 91$ (mod 100).

20. 16

$2^{12} - 1 = (2^6 - 1)(2^6 + 1) = (2^3-1)(2^3+1)(2^6+1) = 7 \cdot 9 \cdot 65 = 3^2 \cdot 5 \cdot 7 \cdot 13$. There are two choices for powers of 3, i.e., $3^1, 3^2$. Also, there are two choices for each 5, 7, and 13, to be either included or excluded in our counts. In other words, there are 2^3 options for 3^n-free factors and 2 options of 3^n. Hence, there are $16(=2^4)$ divisors of $2^{12} - 1$ that are divisible by 3.

REMARKS

- **Legendre's Theorem** : $n(p) = \sum_{k=1}^{\infty} \left\lfloor \dfrac{a}{p^k} \right\rfloor$ from $a!$ where $a, k \in \mathbb{N}$ counts how many primes are multiplied in a factorial. A typical question related to this theorem is terminal zeroes.

- **Fermat's Little Theorem** : $a^{p-1} \equiv 1 \pmod{p}$ where p is a prime and $a \in \mathbb{N}$.

- **Wilson's Theorem** : $(p-1)! \equiv -1 \pmod{p}$.

- **Euler's Totient Function** : $a^{\phi(n)} \equiv 1 \pmod{n}$ where a and n are coprime, and $\phi(n) = n \prod_{p|n}(1 - \dfrac{1}{p})$ where p is a prime factor of n except 1.

- **Euclidean Algorithm** : $\gcd(a, b) = \gcd(b, r_{a,b})$. This resolves GCD of large numbers, e.g.,

$$\begin{aligned}\gcd(2021, 2491) &= \gcd(2021, 2491 - 2021) \\ &= \gcd(2021, 470) \\ &= \gcd(2021 - 470 \cdot 4, 470) \\ &= \gcd(141, 470) \\ &= \gcd(141, 47) \\ &= 47\end{aligned}$$

- Chinese Remainder Theorem : Do not memorize the formula. Just solve the system of equations by substitution. For example, let $x \equiv 2 \pmod{3}$, $x \equiv 3 \pmod{5}$ and $x \equiv 2 \pmod{7}$. Then, $x = 3n_1 + 2 = 5n_2 + 3 = 7n_3 + 2$. If $3n_1 + 2 \equiv 3 \pmod{5}$, then $n_1 = 5p + 2$. Then, $3n^1 + 2 = 15p + 8$, so $15p + 8 \equiv 2 \pmod{7}$. Hence, $p = 7q + 1$. Therefore, $x \equiv 105q + 23$, so $x \equiv 23 \pmod{105 = 3 \times 5 \times 7}$. CRT is used to find out the remainder when a large number is divided out by some large number such as 1000, which comes out oftentimes in AIME. A few more examples will be covered in the next topic.

Legendre's Theorem Proof

From a factorial $a!$, let $n(p^k)$ be the number of multiples of pure exponential primes p^k within $a!$ that can be defined as $\alpha \cdot p^k \neq p^{k+\beta}$ where $k \in \mathbb{N}$. Then,

$$n(p^k) = \left\lfloor \frac{a}{p^k} \right\rfloor - \left\lfloor \frac{a}{p^{k+1}} \right\rfloor$$

Hence,

$$\begin{aligned}
n(p) &= \sum_{k=1}^{\infty} k \left(\left\lfloor \frac{a}{p^k} \right\rfloor - \left\lfloor \frac{a}{p^{k+1}} \right\rfloor \right) \\
&= \left\lfloor \frac{a}{p} \right\rfloor - \left\lfloor \frac{a}{p^2} \right\rfloor + 2\left\lfloor \frac{a}{p^2} \right\rfloor - 2\left\lfloor \frac{a}{p^3} \right\rfloor + 3\left\lfloor \frac{a}{p^3} \right\rfloor - 3\left\lfloor \frac{a}{p^3} \right\rfloor + \cdots \\
&= \left\lfloor \frac{a}{p} \right\rfloor + \left\lfloor \frac{a}{p^2} \right\rfloor + \left\lfloor \frac{a}{p^3} \right\rfloor + \cdots \\
&= \sum_{n=1}^{\infty} \left\lfloor \frac{a}{p^n} \right\rfloor
\end{aligned}$$

 # List of Interesting Polyhedron

Rhombicuboctahedron: The rhombicuboctahedron is a fascinating polyhedron with its mix of square and triangular faces. Its name alone can bring a smile to people's faces due to its complexity and tongue-twisting nature.

Truncated Icosahedron: This polyhedron is famously known as the shape of a traditional soccer ball. Its spherical appearance made up of hexagons and pentagons is both recognizable and aesthetically pleasing.

Dodecahedron: The dodecahedron is another polyhedron that captures attention due to its symmetrical beauty. Its twelve regular pentagonal faces give it a pleasing and harmonious appearance.

Stellated Dodecahedron: By extending the faces of a dodecahedron outward, you get the stellated dodecahedron. Its star-like appearance makes it visually striking and often intriguing to mathematicians and artists alike.

Truncated Tetrahedron: This polyhedron results from cutting off the corners of a tetrahedron. Its triangular and hexagonal faces can create interesting patterns and visual effects.

Great Rhombicosidodecahedron: With its mix of faces including triangles, squares, and pentagons, this polyhedron is a complex and visually captivating shape that can inspire wonder and curiosity.

Snub Cube: The snub cube is derived from the cube by adding pyramids to each face. Its asymmetrical yet balanced appearance can be both surprising and delightful to those who encounter it.

Icosidodecahedron: Combining the properties of an icosahedron and a dodecahedron, this polyhedron features both triangular and pentagonal faces arranged in a symmetrical and harmonious manner.

TOPIC 5

Ending with Number Theory

5.1 Divisibility and Modular Arithmetic
5.2 Chinese Remainder Theorem
5.3 Base Expression and Modular Expression
5.4 Practices

5.1 Divisibility and Modular Arithmetic

Use the following rules when solving competition math questions.

- Divisible by 2 : last digit is even.
- Divisible by 3 : sum of digits is divisible by 3.
- Divisible by 4 : last two digits is multiple of 4.
- Divisible by 5 : last digit is 0 or 5.
- Divisible by 6 : divisible by both 2 and 3.
- Divisible by 8 : last three digits is multiple of 8.
- Divisible by 9 : sum of digits is divisible by 9.
- Divisible by 11 : alternating sum is divisible by 11 (including 0).

Out of all these properties, we must pay attention to divisibility by 9 and 11. Let's have a look at two examples.

Example Is 12345678910111213 divisible by 9?

Solution Convert 12345678910111213 into decimal expressions such that

$$1 \times 10^{15} + 2 \times 10^{14} + \cdots + 9 \times 10^8 + 10 \times 10^6 + 11 \times 10^4 + 12 \times 10^2 + 13$$

Since 10^n can be written as $99\cdots 9 + 1$, we only look at whether the sum of $1, 2, 3, \cdots, 10, 11, 12, 13$ is divisible by 9. Hence,
$1 + 2 + 3 + \cdots + 11 + 12 + 13 = \dfrac{13(1+13)}{2} = 91$ not divisible by 9.

Example Is 12345 divisible by 11?

Solution What does it mean to look at the alternating sum of digits? The alternating sum of digits is $1 - 2 + 3 - 4 + 5 = 9 - 6 = 3$, which is not zero nor divisible by 11. Hence, this is not divisible by 11. Why do we take the alternating sum of digits?

$$\begin{aligned} 12345 &= 1 \times 10000 + 2 \times 1000 + 3 \times 100 + 4 \times 10 + 5 \\ &= 1 \times 9999 + 2 \times 1001 + 3 \times 99 + 4 \times 11 + 5 + (1 - 2 + 3 - 4 + 5) \\ &= 11k + (1 - 2 + 3 - 4 + 5) \\ &= 11k + 3 \end{aligned}$$

which is not a multiple of 11.

Developing bit more than what we covered in the previous topic, we would like to see the properties of modular arithmetic. Instead of giving a gory-detail abstract math, I would like to present you with examples that can be used in competition math.

Example Solve $8n \equiv 4 \pmod{6}$.

Solution Divide $(8, 4, 6)$ by 2 to get $4n \equiv 2 \pmod{3}$. (Here, if $a \equiv b \pmod{n}$, then $\frac{a}{d} \equiv \frac{b}{d} \pmod{\frac{n}{d}}$.) Then, since $4 \equiv 1 \pmod{3}$, $n \equiv 2 \pmod{3}$, so the answer is the set of numbers $\{\cdots, -1, 2, 5, \cdots\}$.

Example Find the smallest positive n such that $3^n \equiv 1 \pmod{10}$.

Solution We will use Euler's Totient Function, i.e., $a^{\phi n} \equiv 1 \pmod{n}$ where a and n are co-prime. We can use ETF, since 3 and 10 are co-prime. First, $\phi(10) = 10(1 - \frac{1}{5})(1 - \frac{1}{2}) = 4$, to find out $3^4 \equiv 1 \pmod{10}$. In fact, we could use $3^1, 3^2, 3^3, 3^4, \cdots$, to find out that remainders are periodic with the period of 4.

Example Solve $3n \equiv 1 \pmod{4}$.

Solution As 3 and 4 are relatively prime, we have $3 \times 3^{-1} \equiv 1 \pmod{4}$ where $3^{-1} \equiv n \pmod{4}$.

$$3n \equiv 1 \pmod{4}$$
$$3n \equiv -3 \pmod{4}$$
$$n \equiv -1 \pmod{4}$$
$$n \equiv 3 \pmod{4}$$

Literally, $3 \times 3 \equiv 1 \pmod{4}$.

5.2 Chinese Remainder Theorem

Chinese Remainder Theorem solves the system of modular equations. Instead of presenting gory details of Chinese Remainder Theorem in abstract language, let's go over two examples to see what it does.

Example If $n \equiv 3 \pmod 5$ and $n \equiv 2 \pmod 7$, find the solution n to the system of modular equations.

Solution First, "$n \equiv 3 \pmod 5$" implies that "$n = 5k + 3$." Hence, "$5k + 3 \equiv 2 \pmod 7$" implies "$5k \equiv -1 \equiv 6 \pmod 7$." Hence, "$5k \equiv 6 \pmod 7$." Therefore, "$k \equiv 4 \pmod 7$." In other words, $k = 7p + 4$ for some integer p. Thus,

$$\begin{aligned} n &= 5k + 3 \\ &= 5(7p + 4) + 3 \\ &= 35p + 20 + 3 \\ &= 35p + 23 \end{aligned}$$

Thus, $n \equiv 23 \pmod{35}$.

5.3 Base Expression and Modular Expression

First, let's look at base expression. Normally, we write a counting number in decimal expression. In other words, we use powers of 10. For example, given $\overline{ABCD}_{10}$, then

$$\overline{ABCD}_{10} = A \times 10^3 + B \times 10^2 + C \times 10 + D$$

where $0 \leq A, B, C, D \leq 9$. How is this connected to modular expression? The first three terms involve powers of 10, so they are multiples of 10. On the other hand, D is stuck between 0 and 9, inclusive. Hence, $\overline{ABCD}_{10} \equiv D \pmod{10}$.

Other than this connection, we need to be able to convert one base number into other base number. Let's have a look at the following example.

Example Convert a counting number 100 into base 7.

Solution First, write down powers of 7 less than or equal to 100, i.e., $7^0, 7^1, 7^2$. Second, divide 100 by the largest powers of 7 in the previous list, 49, to get the remainder of 2. Then, $100 = 2(49) + 2 = 2(7^2) + 0(7^1) + 2 = 202_7$.

Example Convert 1234_5 into a counting number in base 10.

Solution $1234_5 = 1(5^3) + 2(5^2) + 3(5^1) + 4 = 125 + 50 + 15 + 4 = 194$.

When a number is written in base p, we may always convert it into a modular equation with mod p. For instance, if $\overline{ABCD}_P$ is given, then $\overline{ABCD} \equiv D \mod P$. Furthermore, we are allowed to take another step further down into fractions. Recall how decimal expressions are written for fractions. They use up $10^{\text{negative exponent}}$. In other words, 0.12 can be written as $1 \times 10^{-1} + 2 \times 10^{-2}$. Applying this knowledge directly, 0.23_p may be written as $2 \times p^{-1} + 3 \times p^{-2}$. This may bring form either polynomial equation with respect to p or infinite geometric series with the ratio of p.

5.4 Practices

1. Given a five-digit positive palindrome $\overline{ABCBA}$, where A, B and C are each distinct numbers, find the largest possible $\overline{ABCBA}$ divisible by eleven.

> **Walk-Through**
>
> 1. Start with $A = 9$.
>
> 2. Divisibility by 11 implies that the alternating sum of digits is divisible by 11.
>
> 3. Start plugging B values from $B = 8$.
>
> 4. Conclude solving the problem by finding proper values of A, B, and C.

2. A 9-digit number $\overline{PQQPQPQP3}$ is a multiple of 99 for some digits P and Q such that $Q > P$. Find the value of $Q^2 - P^2$.

Walk-Through

1. Divisibility by 9 implies that the sum of all digits is divisible by 9.

2. Divisibility by 11 implies that the alternating sum of all digits is divisible by 11.

3. Try to figure out parities of P and Q. Do they have the same parities or different ones? Reason why they are such.

4. Depending on the answer in step 3, conclude finding the values of P and Q.

3. If there are n positive perfect squares divisible by 8, all of which are less than 500, what is the value of n?

> **Walk-Through**
>
> 1. First, start with a multiple of 8.
>
> 2. Let it be $8k$. Then, $8k$ must be a perfect square.
>
> 3. Find out what goes inside k to amend the problem that 8 has, in terms of perfect squares.
>
> 4. Set up an inequality to find out the number of perfect squares divisible by 8.

4. If $\overline{705A1452B6}$ is a multiple of both 8 and 9, what is the sum of all *distinct* possible values of the product AB?

> **Walk-Through**
>
> 1. Divisibility by 8 implies that the last three digit must form a multiple of 8.
>
> 2. Divisibility by 9 implies that the sum of all digits must be divisible by 9.
>
> 3. Find all possible values of AB. (In fact, there are two distinct values of AB.)

5. Compute $\dfrac{1}{\frac{1}{3}+\frac{1}{5}+\frac{1}{7}}$ (mod 11). (Here, $\dfrac{1}{n} \equiv n^{-1}$ (mod 11).)

> **Walk-Through**
>
> 1. $\dfrac{1}{3} \equiv \dfrac{12}{3}$ (mod 11) because $1 \equiv 12$ (mod 11).
>
> 2. How would one turn $\dfrac{1}{5}$ into other fractions, in mod 11?
>
> 3. Turn $\dfrac{1}{7}$ into another fraction, in mod 11, as well.
>
> 4. Use the same process for the last reciprocal, and conclude solving the problem.

6. For how many integers n satisfying $1 \leq n \leq 23$ is it true that $n^2 \equiv 1 \pmod{24}$?

> **Walk-Through**
>
> 1. For n relatively prime to 24, $n \cdot n^{-1} \equiv 1 \pmod{24}$.
>
> 2. If $n \equiv n^{-1} \pmod{24}$, then $n^2 \equiv 1 \pmod{24}$.
>
> 3. First, find all n such that n and 24 are relatively prime.
>
> 4. Test whether these n values satisfy the given modular equation.

7. Find the smallest positive integer n such that n^{-1} is undefined both (mod 55) and (mod 22).

Walk-Through

1. For n relatively prime to 24, it is true that $n \cdot n^{-1} \equiv 1$ (mod 24).

2. If n^{-1} is undefined for mod 55, it means that n and 55 are not relatively prime.

3. Likewise, if n^{-1} is undefined for mod 22, it means that n and 22 are not relatively prime.

4. Find the smallest common number between step 2 and step 3.

8. Using $35 \cdot 40 = 1400$, **find an integer** n **with** $1399 \leq n < 2798$ **such that** $n \equiv 160^{-1}$ (mod 1399).

Walk-Through

1. Start from $160 \cdot 160^{-1} \equiv 1 \pmod{1399}$.

2. Notice that $1 \equiv 1400 \pmod{1399}$. **In other words,** $160 \cdot 160^{-1} \equiv 1400 \pmod{1399}$.

3. Take out 4 from each side to conclude $40 \cdot 160^{-1} \equiv 400 \pmod{1399}$.

4. Use $35 \cdot 40 \equiv 1 \pmod{1399}$ **to find out** $160^{-1} \pmod{1399}$.

TOPIC 3 Ending with Combinatorics

9. Given that $13^{-1} \equiv 29 \pmod{47}$, find the sum of all possible values of n such that $n \equiv 34^{-1} \pmod{47}$ where $0 \leq n < 94$.

Walk-Through

1. It is true that $34 \cdot 34^{-1} \equiv 1 \pmod{47}$.

2. Check that $n \equiv 34 \pmod{47}$. Multiply -1 to both sides of the equation.

3. $-n \equiv -34 \pmod{47}$. Notice that $-34 \equiv 13 \pmod{47}$.

4. Use $13^{-1} \equiv 29 \pmod{47}$ to solve for n.

10. If $9 \equiv 9^{-1} \pmod{p}$, but $3 \not\equiv 3^{-1} \pmod{p}$, find the number of all possible values of p, where p is a positive integer.

Walk-Through

1. If $9 \equiv 9^{-1} \pmod{p}$, then $81 \equiv 1 \pmod{p}$. Think about why it works this way.

2. If $3 \not\equiv 3^{-1} \pmod{p}$, then $9 \not\equiv 1 \pmod{p}$. Think about why it works this way.

3. Out of all possible values of p, subtract the associated values shown in step 2. Conclude solving the problem.

TOPIC 3 Ending with Combinatorics

11. Suppose $5n \leq 4 \pmod 9$, i.e., $5n \equiv 0 \pmod 9$, $5n \equiv 1 \pmod 9$, $\cdots$, $5n \equiv 4 \pmod 9$. Out of all non-negative integers n from smallest to greatest, what is the 21st number?

Walk-Through

1. If $5n \leq 4 \pmod 9$, then think about how to get rid of 5 in front of n.

2. Find $\dfrac{1}{5} \pmod 9$. Use $1 \equiv 10 \pmod 9$ to find out $5^{-1} \pmod 9$.

3. Now, use it to $5n \equiv k \pmod 9$ where $k = 0, 1, 2, 3,$ and 4 such that $5^{-1}(5n) \equiv 5^{-1}k \pmod 9$.

4. Make sure one write 5 columns of infinitely many integers. Think about why there are 5 columns, instead of 9 columns.

12. What is the product of all positive integer solutions less than or equal to 20 satisfying $39x - 26 \equiv 26 \pmod{8}$?

Walk-Through

1. Notice that $39x \equiv 52 \pmod{8}$.

2. Find the greatest common divisor of 39 and 52.

3. Factor the equation with the greatest common divisor found in step 2.

4. Find $3^{-1} \pmod 8$. Use it to solve for x.

5. Find all possible values of x, and take the product of their values.

13. Suppose k is a multiple of 6. If $k - 2$ is a multiple of n where n is a positive even integer less than 10, then how many possible values are there for n?

Walk-Through

1. Rewrite k into $6x$.

2. $k - 2 \equiv 0 \pmod{n}$, so $6x - 2 \equiv 0 \pmod{n}$.

3. Notice that $6x \equiv 2 \pmod{n}$.

4. Try $n = 2, 4, 6,$ and 8.

5. Conclude solving the problem by finding out some value(s) of n satisfying the given modular equation.

14. There is at least one prime p for which the congruence

$$4x \equiv 1 \pmod{p}$$

has no solution x. Determine the sum of all possible p value(s).

Walk-Through

1. Try $p = 2$. Rewrite $4x \equiv 1 \pmod{2}$, and reason whether there is a solution or not.

2. Try $p = 3$. Do the same thing as step 1.

3. Try $p = 6k + 1$ for some integer k.

4. Try $p = 6k - 1$ for some integer k.

5. Find the value(s) of p such that $4x \equiv 1 \pmod{p}$ has no integer solution.

15. Suppose a prep-book has 136 pages, each of which contains exactly equal number of words. Assuming each page has less than 100 words, the machine that counts the number of words in a whole multiple of 203 gives the remainder of 184. How many words are on each page?

> **Walk-Through**
>
> 1. Let the number of words in each page be n.
>
> 2. The remainder when $136n$ is divided by 203 is 184.
>
> 3. Set up a modular equation in mod 203.
>
> 4. Solve for n.
>
> 5. Make sure that n is smaller than 100, and conclude solving the problem.

16. Bob has seven bags of marbles, each of which contains equal number of marbles. If he adds another bag of 53 marbles, he can redistribute all his marbles so that all eight bags contain exactly equal number of marbles. If he has more than 200 marbles in total, find the smallest number of marbles he had before adding the bag of 53 marbles.

> **Walk-Through**
>
> 1. Seven bags of marbles, each of which contains equal number of marbles, can be written as $7k$ for some integer k.
>
> 2. $7k + 53 \equiv 0 \pmod{8}$, according to the problem.
>
> 3. Since $7k + 53 > 200$, find the smallest possible value of k such that $7k + 53 \equiv 0 \pmod{8}$ and $7k + 53 > 200$, altogether.
>
> 4. Find $7k$, not $7k + 53$, for the final answer to the given problem.

17. Alice thought of a number that is a positive multiple of 6. If she subtracts one, the number turns into a multiple of n. If n is a positive integer less than 10, how many possible values are there for n?

Walk-Through

1. Label a positive multiple of 6 into $6x$.

2. $6x - 1 \equiv 0 \pmod{n}$. Then, $6x \equiv 1 \pmod{n}$.

3. Paraphrase what it means by $6x \equiv 1 \pmod{n}$. Think about $a \cdot a^{-1} \equiv 1 \pmod{n}$ if a and n are relatively prime to one another.

4. Find all possible values of n satisfying such condition.

18. Charlie bought a number of boxes of candles, each of which contains 12 candles. When he took all of the candles out and bundled them into groups of 7, he had two leftover candles. What is the smallest number of boxes of candles he could have bought in the beginning?

> **Walk-Through**
>
> 1. The total number of candles, each of which contains 12 candles, can be written as $12k$.
>
> 2. Paraphrase the next sentence in the problem into modular equation, i.e., $12k \equiv 2 \pmod{7}$.
>
> 3. Solve that modular equation.
>
> 4. Find the exact value of k, not $12k$.

19. There are between 150 and 200 athletes in the gym. Every morning, all athletes gather around the gym, and the head coach separate these individuals into six groups of people. If one athlete is absent, then each group has the same number of athletes. What is the sum of all possible athletes in the gym?

> **Walk-Through**
>
> 1. Let n be the total number of athletes in the gym.
> 2. $n - 1$ is a multiple of 6. Turn it into modular equation.
> 3. Find all possible values of athletes.
> 4. When adding the sum, one may use the formula $\sum_{k=1}^{n} k = \dfrac{n(n+1)}{2}$.

20. Dylan noticed when he stacked his coins in piles of 5, he had 3 left over and when he put them in piles of 7 he had 5 left over. If he has less than 40 coins, how many coins does he have?

> **Walk-Through**
>
> 1. This is a typical Chinese Remainder Theorem. Let n be the number of coins.
>
> 2. $n \equiv 3 \pmod 5$ and $n \equiv 5 \pmod 7$.
>
> 3. One way of solving for n is to write down a list of n values for the first equation and the second equation until the common value is reached.
>
> 4. Another way of solving for n is a method of substitution.
>
> 5. Either by step 3 or 4, find the unique value of n smaller than 40.

21. If n is divided by 4, the remainder is 3. On the other hand, if n is divided by 5, the remainder is 2. Find the closest value of n to 2021.

> **Walk-Through**
>
> 1. Find the modular equations for the first sentence and the second one.
>
> 2. Solve for n.
>
> 3. Find two values of n, one of which is smaller than and another of which is larger than n.
>
> 4. Determine which is closer to 2021, and conclude solving the problem.

22. Find the remainder when

$$\underbrace{1234\cdots 414243444546\cdots 201920202021}_{\text{2021 positive integers from least to greatest}}$$

is divided by 45.

Walk-Through

1. Let N be the given integer.

2. Find $N \pmod 5$, using the divisibility by 5.

3. Find $N \pmod 9$, using the divisibility by 9.

4. Apply Chinese Remainder Theorem on N.

5. The resulting remainder is the answer to the problem.

23. A positive integer n, a multiple of 4, has the remainder of 2 when divided by 3 and the remainder of 5 when divided by 11. If n is between 150 and 250, find the exact value of n.

Walk-Through

1. Notice that $n \equiv 0 \pmod{4}$.

2. Also, $n \equiv 2 \pmod{3}$.

3. Finally, $n \equiv 5 \pmod{11}$.

4. The rule does not change. Rewrite n into $4k$, and substitute $4k$ into step 2 and 3. Solve for k.

5. Now, solve for n. Find the exact value of n.

24. Find the number of ordered natural pairs (r, s) to the equation

$$5r + 3s = 403$$

using modular arithmetic.

> **Walk-Through**
>
> 1. Turn $5r + 3s = 403$ into a modular equation with mod 5.
>
> 2. Likewise, turn it into a modular equation with mod 3.
>
> 3. Solve for r and s, respectively.
>
> 4. Notice that there is one-to-one correspondence between r and s, so use one of the variables to solve for the given equation.

25. In the equation below,
$$123_p + 34_p = 91_{10}.$$
Find the value of p, where p is a positive integer.

> **Walk-Through**
>
> 1. Turn 123_p into counting number in base 10. In particular, $123_p = 1p^2 + 2p + 3$.
>
> 2. Turn 34_p into counting number, as shown in step 1.
>
> 3. 91_{10} is already written in counting number.
>
> 4. Find the value of p by solving for quadratics. Reason why $p > 4$ by making an observation out of 123_p and 34_p.

Answer Key

1. 96569

Since $A - B + C - B + A \equiv 0 \pmod{11}$, we get $2A + C \equiv 2B \pmod{11}$. Substitute $A = 9$ into the equation to maximize $\overline{ABCBA}$. If $A = 9$, then $(B,C) = (8,9), (7,7)$, and $(6,5)$. We stop at $(B,C) = (6,5)$ because $(A,B,C) = (9,6,5)$ produces the largest possible value of 5 digit number divisible by 11.

2. 24

Divisibility by 9 implies that $4P + 4Q \equiv 6 \pmod{9}$. Hence, $P + Q \equiv 6 \pmod{9}$. Likewise, divisibility by 11 implies that $2Q - 2P \equiv -3 \equiv 8 \pmod{11}$. Hence, $Q - P \equiv 4 \pmod{11}$. Thus, $Q = 5, P = 1$. Therefore, $Q^2 - P^2 = 25 - 1 = 24$.

3. 5

Assume that $n = 8(2k^2)$ for some positive integer k. Then, $16k^2 < 500$, by the given assumption. Hence, $k^2 < 31.25$. Therefore, $k = 1, 2, 3, 4, 5$. Thus, there are 5 values of corresponding n values.

4. 59

Multiple of both 8 and 9 imply that $\overline{2B6}$ is divisible by 8 and the sum of digits is also divisible by 9. Hence, $A + B \equiv 6 \pmod{9}$ and $B = 1, 5, 9$ satisfy the first condition. If $B = 1$, then $A = 5$ satisfying $30 + A + B \equiv 0 \pmod{9}$. If $B = 5$, then $A = 1$. Lastly, if $B = 9$, then $A = 6$. Therefore, the sum of all distinct possible values of AB is
$(5)(1) + (6)(9) = 5 + 54 = 59$.

5. 10

First, $3^{-1} \equiv 4 \pmod{11}$ since $3 \cdot 4 \equiv 1 \pmod{11}$. Likewise, $5^{-1} \equiv 9 \pmod{11}$ since $5 \cdot 9 \equiv 1 \pmod{11}$. Lastly, $7^{-1} \equiv 8 \pmod{11}$ since $7 \cdot 8 \equiv 1 \pmod{11}$. Thus, $1/21 = 21^{-1} \equiv 10^{-1} \equiv (-1)^{-1} \equiv 10 \pmod{11}$.

6. 8

The meaning of $n^2 \equiv 1 \pmod{24}$ implies that $n \equiv n^{-1} \pmod{24}$, which further implies that n is relatively prime to 24. Using Euler's totient function, we get

$$\phi(24) = 24(1 - 1/2)(1 - 1/3) = 8.$$

7. 10

If n^{-1} is undefined for $\pmod{55}$, it means that $\gcd(n, 55) \neq 1$. Likewise, if n^{-1} is undefined for $\pmod{22}$, it implies that $\gcd(n, 22) \neq 1$. Hence, the smallest possible value of n satisfying both conditions at the same time is 10.

8. 2457

Since $160^{-1} \cdot 160 \equiv 1 \pmod{1399}$, let $x = 160^{-1}$. Then, $160x \equiv 1 \pmod{1399}$. Hence, $4(40)x \equiv 1 \pmod{1399}$. Multiply 35 to both sides of the equations to get $4x \equiv 35 \pmod{1399}$. Hence, $4x \equiv -1364 \pmod{1399}$. Thus, $x \equiv -341 \pmod{1399}$. $x \equiv 1058 \pmod{1399}$. The answer must be $1058 + 1399 = 2457$.

9. 83

Since $34^{-1} \cdot 34 \equiv 1 \pmod{47}$, let $n = 34^{-1}$. Then, $n \cdot (34 - 47) \equiv 1 \pmod{47}$. Using $13^{-1} \equiv 29 \pmod{47}$, we get $(-29)(-13) \equiv 1 \pmod{47}$. Thus, $n \equiv -29 \equiv 18 \pmod{47}$. Thus, $0 \leq n = 18, 65 < 94$. The sum of all possible values of n is 83.

10. 6

First off, $9 \equiv 9^{-1} \pmod{p}$ implies $9^2 \equiv 1 \pmod{p}$. This means that p divides 80. However, $3 \not\equiv 3^{-1} \pmod{p}$ also implies that p does not divide 8. Thus, out of divisors of 80, we exclude 1, 2, 4 and 8. Hence, there are $p = 5, 10, 16, 20, 40, 80$.

11. 36

First $5n \equiv k \pmod{9}$ can be converted into $10n \equiv n \equiv 2k \pmod{9}$. Thus, $n \equiv 0, 2, 4, 6, 8 \pmod{9}$. Listing the numbers from the smallest positive integer, we get $\{0, 2, 4, 6, 8, 9, 11, \cdots, 31, 33, 35, 36 \cdots\}$. 21'st number in the list is 36.

12. 960

Since $39x \equiv 52 \pmod{8}$, we simplify the equation into $3x \equiv 4 \pmod{8}$. Hence, $x \equiv 4 \pmod{8}$. Thus, $x = 4, 12, 20$. The product of these three values is 960.

13. 3

Let $k = 6x$ for some integer x. Then, $k - 2 = 6x - 2 \equiv 0 \pmod{n}$ for some positive even n. Then, $6x \equiv 2 \pmod{n}$. Out of positive even numbers less than 10, n cannot be 6 because the left-side turns into 0 whereas 2 is not equivalent to 0 mod n. Hence, $n = 2, 4, 8$. There are three possible values.

14. 2

Since $2x \equiv 1 \pmod{p}$, the leftside of the equation is a multiple of 2 whereas the rightside is not. Rewriting $2x = pk + 1$ for some k, we get p as either 2 or odd primes. If p is odd, then both sides of the equation are even. However, if $p = 2$, then $2(x - k) = 1$ for some integer x and k, which is not possible. Hence, there is only one value of p, i.e., 2.

15. 73

Solving $136n \equiv 184 \pmod{203}$, we get $-67n \equiv -19 \pmod{203}$. Hence, $67n \equiv 19 \pmod{203}$. Thus, $201n \equiv 57 \pmod{203}$. This implies that $-2n \equiv 57 \pmod{203}$. Thus, $-2n \equiv -146 \pmod{203}$. Therefore, there are 73 words in each page.

16. 203

Let b be the smallest number of coins you have before finding the bag of 53 coins. Then, $7b+53 \equiv 0 \pmod 8$. Hence, $7b \equiv -5 \pmod 8$. Therefore, $b \equiv 5 \pmod 8$. Since $b = 8n+5$ and $7b+53 > 200$ implies $b > 21$, we get $b = 29$ as the smallest possible value. Thus, $29 \cdot 7 = 203$.

17. 3

Let $6k-1 \equiv 0 \pmod n$. Then, $6k \equiv 1 \pmod n$. This implies that $\gcd(6,n)=1$. Hence, there are $n=1,5,7$. Thus, there are three possible values of n.

18. 6

Let n be the number of boxes of candles he bought in the beginning. Then, $12n \equiv 2 \pmod 7$ implies $6n \equiv 1 \pmod 7$. Hence, $-n \equiv 1 \pmod 7$. Thus, $n \equiv 6 \pmod 7$. Therefore, the smallest possible value of n is 6.

19. 1575

Let n be the number of athletes in each group. Then, $n-1 \equiv 0 \pmod 6$. Therefore, $n \equiv 1 \pmod 6$. This implies that $150 < 6n+1 < 200$. The sum of all possible values of total number of athletes is

$$\frac{9(151+199)}{2} = 1575$$

20. 33

Let n be the number of coins Dylan has. Then, $n \equiv 3 \pmod 5$ and $n \equiv 5 \pmod 7$ at the same time. Hence, $n = 5k+3$ for some k. Thus, $5k+3 \equiv 5 \pmod 7$. Therefore, $5k \equiv 2 \pmod 7$. This is equivalent to $5k \equiv -5 \pmod 7$. Thus, $k \equiv -1 \pmod 7$. In other words, $k = 7q+6$. Thus, $n = 5(7q+6)+3 = 35q+33$. Hence, the smallest positive n is 33.

21. 2027

$n \equiv 3 \pmod 4$ and $n \equiv 2 \pmod 5$. Hence, $n = 4k+3$ for some integer k. Thus, $4k+3 \equiv 2 \pmod 5$. Hence, $4k \equiv -1 \pmod 5$. It is conclusive that $k \equiv 1 \pmod 5$. Thus, $n = 4(5q+1)+3$ for some integer q. Thus, $n = 20q+7$. The closest value of n to 2021 is 2027.

22. 6

Let this number be n. Then, it is obvious that $n \equiv 1 \pmod 5$ and $n \equiv 6 \pmod 9$. Then, $n = 9k+6$. Thus, $9k+6 \equiv 1 \pmod 5$ implies $9k \equiv -5 \pmod 5$. Hence, $k \equiv 0 \pmod 5$. Thus, $n = 9(5q)+6 = 45q+6$. The remainder must be 6.

23. 236

$n \equiv 0 \pmod 4$, $n \equiv 2 \pmod 3$ and $n \equiv 5 \pmod{11}$ at the same time. Let $n = 4k$ for some k. Then, $4k \equiv 2 \pmod 3$ implies $k \equiv 2 \pmod 3$. let $k = 3q + 2$. Then, $n = 12q + 8$. hence, $12q + 8 \equiv 5 \pmod{11}$. Then, $q \equiv -3 \pmod{11}$. Thus, $q \equiv 8 \pmod{11}$. Therefore, $n = 12(11r + 8) + 8 = 132r + 104$. Therefore, $n = 236$.

24. 27

Turn $5r + 3s = 403$ into modular equation - $2r \equiv 1 \pmod 3$. Then, $r \equiv 2 \pmod 3$. Also, since r and s are natural pairs, we get $5r \leq 400$. Hence, $r \leq 80$. Therefore, $r = 2, 5, \cdots, 77, 80$ implies that there are 27 possible values of r. Each value of r determines unique value of s, so there are 27 pairs of (r, s) satisfying $5r + 3s = 403$.

25. 7

Since $p^2 + 2p + 3 + 3p + 4 = 91$ where $p > 4$, we get $p^2 + 5p - 84 = 0$. Hence, $p = -12$ or $p = 7$. The only possible value of p must be 7.

TOPIC 6

Beginning with Geometry

6.1 Basic Guidelines for Plane Geometry Problems

6.2 Angle Bisector and Perpendicular Bisector

6.3 Practices

6.1 Basic Guidelines for Plane Geometry Problems

When we solve plane geometry questions, always remember the following rules.

- Label relevant information.

- Set up proper equations or expressions.

You need courage to label pieces of information and write the equation when you see geometry questions. What kinds of equations or expressions do we use most in geometry questions in competition math?

- Pythagoras Theorem (associated with auxiliary perpendicular lines)

- Similar Triangles (associated with auxiliary parallel lines or AA similarity ratio)

- Base ratio = Area ratio (with fixed height)

- Laws of Cosines (in AMC 12 and above)

Pythagoras Theorem with Auxiliary Perpendicular Lines

Definition: The Pythagoras Theorem states that in a right triangle, the square of the length of the hypotenuse (c) is equal to the sum of the squares of the lengths of the other two sides (a and b):

$$c^2 = a^2 + b^2$$

Application with Auxiliary Perpendicular Lines: In competition problems, the Pythagoras Theorem can be extended by drawing auxiliary perpendicular lines to create right triangles. This often helps in decomposing complex figures into simpler right triangles for which the Pythagoras Theorem can be applied directly or indirectly.

Similar Triangles with Auxiliary Parallel Lines or AA Similarity

Definition: Two triangles are similar if their corresponding angles are equal (Angle-Angle or AA similarity) and their corresponding sides are proportional.
Formal Condition: For triangles $\triangle ABC$ and $\triangle DEF$,

$$\angle A = \angle D, \angle B = \angle E \implies \triangle ABC \sim \triangle DEF$$

Application with Auxiliary Parallel Lines: Drawing auxiliary parallel lines can help in identifying similar triangles within a geometric figure. Parallel lines create corresponding angles, leading to AA similarity and allowing the use of proportional relationships between corresponding sides.

Base Ratio Equals Area Ratio (with Fixed Height)

Definition: In triangles sharing the same height, the ratio of their areas is equal to the ratio of their bases.

Formal Condition: For triangles $\triangle ABC$ and $\triangle DEF$ with the same height h from vertices A and D to bases BC and EF, respectively,

$$\frac{\text{Area of } \triangle ABC}{\text{Area of } \triangle DEF} = \frac{BC}{EF}$$

Application: This principle is useful in problems where triangles have a common altitude, allowing simplification of area comparisons to base comparisons.

Law of Cosines

Definition: The Law of Cosines relates the lengths of the sides of a triangle to the cosine of one of its angles. For any triangle $\triangle ABC$ with sides a, b, and c, and the angle θ opposite side c,

$$c^2 = a^2 + b^2 - 2ab\cos(\theta)$$

Applications: The Law of Cosines is particularly useful in competition problems to:

- Determine the third side of a triangle when two sides and the included angle are known.

- Calculate angles when all three sides of a triangle are known.

- Generalize the Pythagoras Theorem to non-right triangles.

Similar triangles deal with more theorems such as

- Ceva's Theorem : cevians are line segments connecting a vertex to any point on the opposite side.

- Menelaus Theorem : if three points are collinear, always drop an altitude from the other vertices not on the line containing these three points.

whereas "base ratio = area ratio" deals with

- Median property of $2:1$ ratio

- Angle bisector property

The key idea about finding other pieces of information from the figure is to use the following method.

- Drop an altitude : it automatically forms a right triangle, meaning that we may figure out either height or the area.

- Draw a parallel line : its purpose is to figure out AA similarity. Usually, parallel lines are connected with alternate interior angles, and sometimes with isosceles triangles.

Example Given a triangle ABC, there exists a point D on $\overline{BC}$ such that $BD:CD = 3:1$. Find the area ratio between ABD and ACD.

Solution Notice that ABD and ACD are non-similar figures. In other words, we use the base ratio to solve for the problem.

Let $BD = 3k$ and $CD = k$. Also, denote its height as h. Then, $[ABD] = \frac{1}{2}(3k)h$ and $[ACD] = \frac{1}{2}(k)h$, so the area ratio equals the base ratio $3:1$.

6.2 Angle Bisector and Perpendicular Bisector

Angle bisector is the set of points equidistant from two distinct intersecting lines. Perpendicular bisector, on the other hand, is the set of points equidistant from two distinct points. What are the important features about angle bisector and perpendicular bisector?

- Isosceles triangle : the angle bisector of a vertex angle coincides with the perpendicular bisector of the opposite side.

- Angle bisector : angle bisectors of a triangle meet at a point called *incenter*. It forms a circle inscribed within the triangle. In order to find the length of inradius, we use two methods - area method or length method. Area method is used when the sides are all integers, and length method are used when the triangle is right triangle. However, if all sides have non-integer sides and the triangle is not right, then we use Pythagoras theorem to use area method.

- Perpendicular bisector : perpendicular bisectors of a triangle meet at a point (possibly outside the triangle) called *circumcenter*. It forms a circle circumscribing the given triangle. In order to find the circumcenter, we may need to use laws of sines, i.e.,

$$\frac{a}{\sin(A)} = \frac{b}{\sin(B)} = \frac{c}{\sin(C)} = 2R$$

where R is the circumradius.

Example Find the inradius of a triangle with side lengths 3, 4, and 5.

Solution For learning purpose, let's focus on the area method. If there is the incenter I, cut the right triangle into three triangles that could be attached to form the original triangle, each of which share a vertex at I. Then, the area of the triangle is $\frac{1}{2} \times 3 \times 4 = 6$, whereas the area can also be written as $\frac{1}{2}(3 + 4 + 5)r$. Hence, $r = 1$.

Example Find the inradius of a triangle with side lengths 5, 6, and 7.

Solution This is not a right triangle. However, we use exactly equivalent method. If there is the incenter I, cut the right triangle into three triangles that could be attached to form the original triangle, each of which share a vertex at I. Then, the area of the triangle is $\sqrt{9(9-5)(9-6)(9-7)} = 6\sqrt{6}$[1], whereas the area can also be written as $\frac{1}{2}(5 + 6 + 7)r$. Hence, $r = \frac{2\sqrt{6}}{3}$.

[1] This is called Heron's formula, which is used when side lengths are integers(or some rationals), i.e., $A = \sqrt{s(s-a)(s-b)(s-c)}$ for $s = \frac{a+b+c}{2}$

6.3 Practices

1. In triangle ABC, the angle bisectors are $\overline{AD}$, $\overline{BE}$, and $\overline{CF}$, which intersect at the incenter I. If $\angle ABC = 38°$, then find the measure of $\angle CID$.

> **Walk-Through**
>
> 1. Label each of the angles, according to the angle bisector information.
>
> 2. Set up an angle equation - the interior angle sum theorem of a triangle.
>
> 3. Chase angles with the exterior angle theorem.
>
> 4. Find the measure of $\angle CID$.

2. Find the inradius of the circle inscribed in triangle PQR if $PR = 15$, $PQ = 41$, and $QR = 52$.

Walk-Through

1. Using angle bisectors of each interior angle, find the incenter.

2. Find the area of a triangle PQR by using either Pythagorean Theorem or Heron's formula.

3. Use the formula Area $= sr$ where s is the semiperimeter and r is the inradius.

4. Conclude the problem by finding the length of inradius.

3. The triangle $\triangle PQR$ is an isosceles triangle where $PQ = 4\sqrt{2}$ and $\angle Q$ is a right angle. If I is the incenter of $\triangle PQR$, then what is the length QI, in the form $a + b\sqrt{c}$, where a, b, and c are integers, and c is not divisible by any perfect square other than 1?

> **Walk-Through**
>
> 1. Apply the same logic as the previous problem.
>
> 2. Perform length-chasing by labeling the tangent lengths.
>
> 3. Remember that a point off the circle produces two congruent tangents to the circle.
>
> 4. Find the inradius, and use the right isosceles triangle property to find out the length QI.

4. In triangle PQR, $PQ = PR$ and S is a point on $\overline{PR}$ so that $\overline{QS}$ bisects angle $\angle PQR$. If $QS = QR$, what is the measure, in degrees, of the vertex angle P?

> **Walk-Through**
>
> 1. Perform angle-chasing by labeling the angle measures properly.
>
> 2. This is a famous triangle for golden ratio. Algebra 2 / Precalculus topic will cover this triangle in depth to figure out the measure of $\cos(36°)$.

5. Let $\triangle PQR$ be an isosceles triangle such that $QR = 30$ and $PQ = PR$. We have that I is the incenter of $\triangle PRQ$, and $IR = 18$. What is the length of the inradius of the triangle?

Walk-Through

1. Remember that the perpendicular bisector of the base of an isosceles triangle is equivalent to the angle bisector of the vertex angle of the triangle.

2. Let the midpoint of $\overline{QR}$ be M.

3. Set up a Pythaogrean equation for right triangle MRI.

4. Solve for the inradius.

6. In triangle PQR, $PQ = 16$, $PR = 24$, $QR = 19$, and PS is an angle bisector. Find the ratio of the area of triangle PQS to the area of triangle PRS.

> **Walk-Through**
>
> 1. According to the Angle Bisector Theorem, the side ratio equals the base ratio and the area ratio.
>
> 2. Use PQ and PR to set up the base ratio.
>
> 3. Let the height from P to $\overline{QR}$ be h.
>
> 4. Find the ratio of $[PQS]$ to $[PRS]$, using the base ratio and h. Notice that this matches with step 1.

7. Given a right triangle ABC, where P is the point on hypotenuse $\overline{AC}$ such that $\angle ABP = 45°$. Given that $AP = 3$ and $CP = 4$, compute the area of ABC.

> **Walk-Through**
>
> 1. Notice that $\angle ABP = 45°$ is a great way to hide the angle bisector theorem.
>
> 2. Apply the Angle Bisector Theorem to label two sides with $AP : CP$. In particular, label AB and BC with letter k.
>
> 3. Express AC with k.
>
> 4. Use $AC = 7$ to figure out the exact value of k.
>
> 5. Uset step 4 to find out the area of triangle ABC.

8. Given two right triangles CAB and DBA sharing a side $\overline{AB}$,

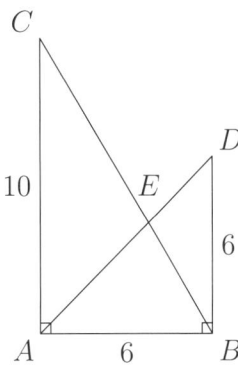

what is the area of $\triangle ABE$?

Walk-Through

1. The bottom line for this problem is that we use either similarity or angle bisector theorem.

2. First, in order to use similarity, drop the altitude from E to $\overline{AB}$, and label it.

3. Second, in order to use the angle bisector theorem, label CE and BE, using $AC : AB$.

4. Either by step 2 or 3, find the area of $\triangle ABE$.

9. In triangle ABC, $AB = 13$, $AC = 14$, and $BC = 15$. Let I be the incenter. The incircle of triangle ABC touches sides BC, AC, and AB at D, E, and F, respectively. Find the length of BI.

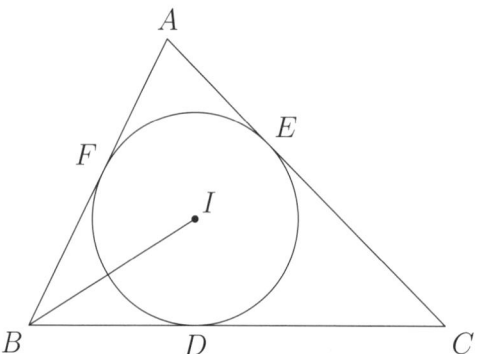

Walk-Through

1. Notice that the area of triangle ABC is 84.

2. Perform length-chasing for BD. Check that $BD = BF$, $AF = AE$, and $CE = CD$.

3. Find the inradius of triangle ABC.

4. Use Pythagorean Theorem for triangle BID to find the length of BI.

10. In triangle ABC, let angle bisectors $\overline{BD}$ and $\overline{CE}$ intersect at I. The line through I parallel to $\overline{BC}$ intersects $\overline{AB}$ and $\overline{AC}$ at P and Q, respectively. If $AB = 19$, $AC = 25$, and $BC = 33$, then find the perimeter of triangle APQ.

Walk-Through

1. Underline "parallel," and use the alternate interior angle theorem to label angles.

2. Use the converse of isosceles triangle theorem to find congruent sides.

3. Notice that the perimeter of APQ can be found by the side lengths of ABC.

11. Let $\triangle PQR$ have side lengths $PQ = 13$, $PR = 14$, and $QR = 15$. There are two circles located inside $\angle QPR$ which are tangent to rays $\overrightarrow{PQ}$, $\overrightarrow{PR}$, and segment $\overline{QR}$. Let S be the center of incircle within $\triangle PQR$ and L be the center of the circle tangent to $\overrightarrow{PQ}$, $\overrightarrow{PR}$ and segment $\overline{QR}$, but outside $\triangle PQR$. Find the difference between the two radii.

> **Walk-Through**
>
> 1. Draw a triangle PQR.
>
> 2. Label S, its incenter.
>
> 3. Label L, its excenter.
>
> 4. It is easy to find out the length of inradius.
>
> 5. Find the radius of the excircle of P.
>
> 6. Use labeling and similarity to find the difference between the two radii.

12. In triangle PQR, where Q is the right angle, and point S lies on segment PR such that QS is an angle bisector of $\angle PQR$. If $PQ = 35$ and $QR = 14$, then find SR.

Walk-Through

1. Angle bisector theorem states that the side ratio equals the base ratio.

2. Produce a prototype right triangle for $2 : 5 : \sqrt{29}$.

3. Use step 2 to figure out the length SR.

13. In triangle ABC, $AB = 13$, $AC = 14$, and $BC = 15$. Let I be the incenter. The incircle of triangle ABC touches the triangle at D, E, and F, as shown in the figure. Find the area of concave pentagon $BFIEC$.

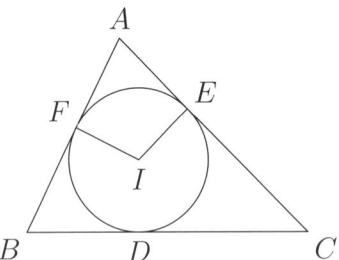

Walk-Through

1. Find the length $AF(= AE)$.

2. Find $IF(= IE)$.

3. Notice that this is a kite.

4. Find the area of $AFIE$.

5. Take $[AFIE]$ from $[ABC]$ to conclude finding the area of $BFIEC$.

14. We have a scalene triangle $\triangle PQR$ such that $PQ = 5$, $PR = 4$, and $QR = 6$. If PS is an angle bisector such that S is on QR, then find the value of PS^2.

Walk-Through

1. In order to solve this problem, one may use Stewart's Theorem or Pythagorean Theorem.

2. In this walk-through, use Stewart's Theorem.

3. Let $PQ = c$, $PR = b$, $QS = m$, $SR = n$, $PS = d$, and $QR = a$. Stewart's Theorem states $m \cdot a \cdot n + d \cdot a \cdot d = b \cdot m \cdot b + c \cdot n \cdot c$.

4. Use step 3 to find PS^2.

15. In triangle ABC, $\angle BAC = 76°$. The incircle of triangle ABC touches sides BC, AC, and AB at D, E, and F, respectively. Find the measure of $\angle FDE$, in degrees.

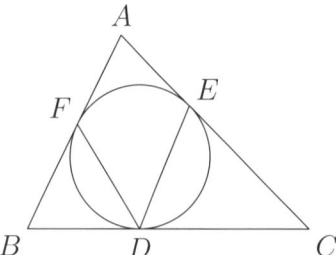

Walk-Through

1. Notice that $\triangle BFD$ is isosceles.

2. Likewise, $\triangle CDE$ is isosceles.

3. Locate the incenter, and connect it to F and E, respectively.

4. There are two ways of solving for $m\angle FDE$. First, labeling B and C, and angle-chasing for $m\angle FDE$. Second, use the ratio between the inscribed angle and the central angle.

5. Use step 4 to find out the measure of $\angle FDE$.

16. Given an isosceles triangle ABC, where $AB = AC = 5$ and $BC = 6$, let O be the circumcenter of triangle ABC. Find the circumference of the circle centered at O circumscribing $\triangle ABC$.

Walk-Through

1. Out of many ways to solve for circumradius, use Pythagorean Theorem.

2. Drop the altitude from A to $\overline{BC}$.

3. Let R be the circumradius of ABC.

4. Set up Pythagorean Theorem to find R.

5. Find πR^2 and conclude solving the problem.

17. Triangle ABC with $AB : AC = 5 : 1$ has area 12. Let D be the midpoint of $\overline{AB}$, and let E be the midpoint of $\overline{AC}$. The angle bisector of $\angle BAC$ intersects $\overline{DE}$ and $\overline{BC}$ at F and G, respectively. What is the area of quadrilateral $FECG$?

> **Walk-Through**
>
> 1. Use angle bisector theorem to find the base ratio using $AB : AC = 5 : 1$.
>
> 2. Find $[AGC]$.
>
> 3. Find $EF : GC$ in order to find the area ratio $[AFI] : [AGC]$.
>
> 4. Hence, find $[FECG]$.

18. Triangle ABC has a right angle at B, $AB = 1$, and $BC = 3$. The bisector of $\angle BAC$ meets $\overline{BC}$ at D. What is BD?

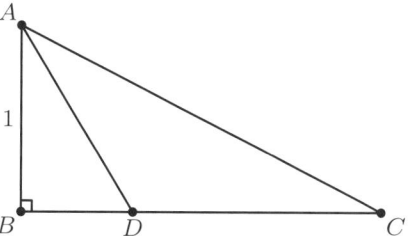

Walk-Through

1. Find AC, using Pythagorean Theorem.

2. Find $BD : CD$ by angle bisector theorem.

3. Use the segment addition postulate to solve for BD.

19. Triangle ABC with $AB : AC = 5 : 3$ has area 24. Let D be the midpoint of $\overline{AB}$, and let E be the midpoint of $\overline{AC}$. The angle bisector of $\angle BAC$ intersects $\overline{DE}$ and $\overline{BC}$ at F and G, respectively. Find the ratio of $[DFG] : [AFE]$.

Walk-Through

1. Find $BG : GC$ by angle bisector theorem.

2. Find $[ABG]$.

3. Hence, find $[DFG]$ and $[AGC]$.

4. Use similarity ratio to find out $[AFE]$.

5. Hence, find the ratio $[DFG] : [AFE]$.

20. In a parallelogram $ABCD$, there exists a point P on the line containing BC such that $\overline{DP}$ intersects with the segment $\overline{AB}$ at Q. Let R be the intersection point between $\overline{DP}$ and $\overline{AC}$. Then, D, R, Q, and P are collinear. If $PQ = 4$ and $RQ = 3$, find DR.

> **Walk-Through**
>
> 1. Label DR and AQ with different letters.
>
> 2. Use similar figures to set up two similarity ratio, since there are two letters.
>
> 3. Get rid of AQ using substitution to find the length DR.

TOPIC 3 Ending with Combinatorics 215

Answer Key

1. $71°$

Let $m\angle ACI = y$ and $m\angle IAC = x$. Then, $2x + 2y + 38° = 180°$. Hence, $2x + 2y = 142°$. This implies that $x + y = 71°$.

2. $\dfrac{13}{3}$

Use Heron's Formula. Compute the semi-perimeter, i.e.,
$$S = \dfrac{15 + 41 + 52}{2} = 54$$

Then,
$$A = \sqrt{S(S-a)(S-b)(S-c)}$$
$$= \sqrt{54 \cdot 2 \cdot 13 \cdot 39}$$
$$= 13 \cdot 18$$

Hence, $54r = 13 \cdot 18$, so $r = \dfrac{13}{3}$.

3. $8 - 4\sqrt{2}$

Instead of using Heron's formula, since the triangle is a right triangle, let the radius be r. Then, $4\sqrt{2} - r + 4\sqrt{2} - r = 8$. Hence, $r = 4\sqrt{2} - 4$. Since $QI = \sqrt{2}r$, we get $QI = 8 - 4\sqrt{2}$.

4. 36

Let x be the angle measure of P. Then, $\triangle PSQ$ is an isosceles triangle to conclude that $m\angle SQP = x$. Thus, $m\angle QSR = 2x$. By assumption, we also conclude that $m\angle R = 2x$. Thus, the sum of interior angles for triangle PQR is equal to $x + 2x + 2x = 5x$. Thus, $x = 36$, in degree.

5. $3\sqrt{11}$

Since $\triangle PQR$ is an isosceles triangle, let S be the midpoint of $\overline{QR}$. Hence, $QS = SR = 15$. Using Pythagorean theorem, we conclude that $IS^2 + 15^2 = IR^2 = 18^2$. Thus, $IS^2 = 18^2 - 15^2 = (18-15)(18+15) = 99$. Thus, $IS = 3\sqrt{11}$.

6. $\dfrac{2}{3}$

Using Angle Bisector Theorem, we conclude that $QS : SR = 2 : 3$. Let, $QX = 2k$ and $SR = 3k$ for some real number k. Since Q, S, and R are collinear, $\triangle PQS : \triangle PRS$ is equal to the base length ratio, i.e., $2 : 3$.

7. $\dfrac{294}{25}$

Since $AP : PC = AB : BC$ by angle bisector theorem, let $AB = 3k$ and $BC = 4k$ for some real k. Then, $AC = 5k$ by Pythagorean Theorem. Hence, $5k = 7$. Now, the area of triangle ABC equals
$$\dfrac{1}{2} \cdot (3k) \cdot (4k) = 6k^2$$
$$= 6(\dfrac{7}{5})^2$$
$$= \dfrac{294}{25}$$

8. $\dfrac{45}{4}$

Since $\overline{AC} \parallel \overline{BD}$, we use similar triangles. The length ratio of ACE to BDE is $5 : 3$. Hence, the area of $\triangle ACE = \dfrac{1}{2} \cdot 10 \cdot \dfrac{15}{4} = \dfrac{75}{4}$. Thus, the area of $\triangle ABE$ is equal to $30 - \dfrac{75}{4} = \dfrac{45}{4}$.

9. $\sqrt{65}$

It is easy to check that $BF = BD = 7$, $AF = AE = 6$ and $CE = CD = 8$. Using Heron's formula, we conclude that the area is $84 = \sqrt{21 \cdot 8 \cdot 7 \cdot 6}$. Hence, $IF = 84/s = 4$. Using Pythagorean Theorem, we conclude that the $IB = \sqrt{7^2 + 4^2} = \sqrt{65}$.

10. 44

The perimeter of $\triangle APQ$ is equal to $AB + AC$ since $IP = PB$ and $IQ = CQ$ due to parallel line property and converse of isosceles triangle theorem. Hence, $19 + 25 = 44$.

11. 10

The radius of an inscribed circle of PQR is 4. On the other hand, we need to find the larger radius. Since L, S and P are collinear due to the definition of angle bisector, and the larger circle centered at excenter-P, we have two similar right triangles whose hypotenuses are $\overline{PS}$ and $\overline{PL}$, respectively, with the ratio of $6 : 21$. Since the inradius is 4, we get the larger radius as 14. Hence, the difference between the two radii is 10.

12. $2\sqrt{29}$

By angle bisector theorem, we get $PQ : QR = PS : SR = 5 : 2$. Let $PS = 5k$ and $SR = 2k$ for some real number k. Also, $PR = 7\sqrt{5^2 + 2^2} = 7\sqrt{29}$, by Pythagorean Theorem. Hence, $SR = 2\sqrt{29}$.

13. 60

Since $IF = IE = 4$, and $m\angle AFI = m\angle AEI = 90$, the area of $AEIF = 24$. Since the area of triangle $ABC = 84$, the area of pentagon $BFIEC = 84 - 24 = 60$.

14. $\dfrac{100}{9}$

By angle bisector theorem, $QS : SR = 5 : 4$, and $QS = 10/3$ and $SR = 8/3$. Hence, using Stewart's Theorem,

$$\frac{10}{3} \cdot \frac{8}{3} \cdot 6 + 6 \cdot PS^2 = 16 \cdot \frac{10}{3} + 25 \cdot \frac{8}{3}$$
$$\frac{160}{3} + 6PS^2 = \frac{360}{3}$$
$$PS^2 = \frac{100}{9}$$

15. $52°$

Let I be the incenter. Then, $m\angle FIE = 104°$, since $AFIE$ is cyclic. Since $\angle FDE$ is an inscribed angle for central angle of measure $104°$, we conclude that $m\angle FDE = 52°$.

16. $\dfrac{25\pi}{4}$

Let r be the circumradius of $\triangle ABC$. Since $\triangle ABC$ is isosceles, we use Pythagorean Theorem.

$$r^2 = 3^2 + (4-r)^2$$
$$r^2 = 9 + 16 - 8r + r^2$$
$$25 = 8r$$
$$\frac{25}{8} = r$$

TOPIC 3 Ending with Combinatorics 217

17. $\dfrac{3}{2}$

Since $BG : GC = 5 : 1$, we get $[\triangle AGC]$ as $\dfrac{1}{6} \cdot [ABC]$. Also, since $EF : GC = 1 : 2$, the area ratio between $\triangle AFI$ and $\triangle AGC$ is $1 : 4$. Thus,

$$[FECG] = 12 \times \dfrac{1}{6} \times \dfrac{3}{4} = \dfrac{3}{2}$$

18. $\dfrac{\sqrt{10} - 1}{3}$

Since $AC = \sqrt{AB^2 + BC^2} = \sqrt{10}$, we conclude that $BD : DC = 1 : \sqrt{10}$, by angle bisector theorem. Hence, $BD = k$ and $DC = \sqrt{10}k$ for some real k. Hence, $(1 + \sqrt{10})k = 3$ implies that $BD = k = \dfrac{\sqrt{10} - 1}{3}$.

19. $\dfrac{5}{3}$

Use $BG : GC = 5 : 3$ to conclude that $[ABG] = 24 \cdot 5/8 = 15$. Hence, $[DFG] = 15 \cdot 1/2 \cdot 1/2 = 15/4$. Likewise, $[AGC] = 24 \cdot 3/8 = 9$. Hence, $[AFE] = 9 \times 1/4 = 9/4$. Thus, the ratio $[DFG] : [AFE] = 15 : 9 = 5 : 3$.

20. $\sqrt{21}$

Let $DR = x$ and $AQ = k$. Then, $AQ : CD = QR : RD$, so $CD = \dfrac{xk}{3}$. Hence, $BQ = k(\dfrac{x}{3} - 1)$. By similarity, $PQ : PD = BQ : CD$, so $(7 + x)(\dfrac{x}{3} - 1) = \dfrac{4}{3}x$. Hence, $x^2 = 21$, so $x = \sqrt{21}$.

TOPIC 7

Ending with Geometry

7.1 Quadrilaterals and Cyclic Quadrilaterals

7.2 Circles

7.3 Practices

7.1 Quadrilaterals and Cyclic Quadrilaterals

When we see quadrilaterals, we always have to think in terms of diagonals.

- Isosceles trapezoid has congruent diagonals.
- Parallelogram has diagonals bisected.
- Rectangle has congruent diagonals bisected.
- Rhombus has perpendicular diagonals bisected.
- Square has congruent diagonals perpendicularly bisected.

Normally, quadrilaterals can be solved by cutting the figure into triangles, since triangles consist of all planar polygons. On the other hand, if there are cyclic quadrilaterals[1], we employ the following strategies when solving such questions.

- **Inscribed angles** of equal intercepted arcs are equal, forming **similar triangles**.
- **Opposite angles** of quadrilateral are **supplementary**, asking us to use **Laws of Cosines**.
- **Two chords** intersecting inside the cyclic quadrilateral can be written as **power of points**.

Special theorems associated to cyclic quadrilaterals can be laid out as

- **Ptolemy** Theorem : the sum of the product of two opposite sides equals the product of diagonals. The proof requires **similar triangles**.
- **Brahmagupta's** Theorem : the **area of a cyclic quadrilateral** is an extension of Heron's formula where the area equals

$$\sqrt{(s-a)(s-b)(s-c)(s-d)}$$

where $s = \dfrac{a+b+c+d}{2}$.

---

[1]Cyclic quadrilateral is a quadrilateral that has a circumscribing circle.

7.2 Circles

Circle is the set of points equidistant from a particular fixed point, known as its center. Due to its equidistant property, the circle automatically involves isosceles triangles. However, the most common type of questions related to circle questions is the external tangency question. Here are the rules we can follow when we see circles.

- If you see **a chord inside the circle**, draw a **perpendicular bisector**. There must be a center at that perpendicular bisector.

- If two circles are **externally tangent**, then always connect the centers. You will use **Pythagoras Theorem** because tangent line is perpendicular to the center. Sometimes, you may need to use **similar triangles**.

- If the circle is given in the **coordinate plane**, always draw **horizontal and vertical lines** passing through the centers. Even when it is not in the coordinate plane, it is always useful to draw auxiliary lines to form right triangles for equations. Remember that we need to label the figures to come up with equations.

Most of the circle questions, other than externally tangent circles, you may have to use the laws of cosines. In fact, many challenging questions related to geometry questions can be solved by applying laws of cosines. Here is the second law of cosines for a triangle ABC, with $AB = c$, $AC = b$ and $CB = a$, i.e.

$$a^2 = b^2 + c^2 - 2bc\cos(A)$$

So far, we have been looking at plane geometry tools, but some questions may involve more tools other than geometrical tools. The following strategy shows a typical thinking process for geometry questions. In this section, we will mainly focus on plane geometry.

- Plane Geometry : Pythagoras, AA similarity, and base ratio=area ratio.

- Coordinate Geometry : Put everything in coordinate plane for bashing method. Some people call it analytic geometry. AMC 12 or AIME so far have asked students about analytic geometry in intermediate level questions.

- Trigonometry : Sometimes the question might be solved easier if we put everything in complex plane or use vectors to solve rotational geometry questions.

7.3 Practices

1. In the diagram, $PQRS$ is a trapezoid with an area of 24. RS is twice the length of PQ. What is the area of $\triangle SQR$?

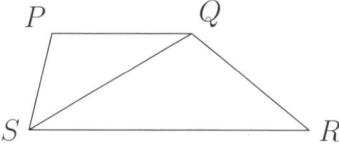

Walk-Through

1. Notice that a trapezoid has the same height.

2. The area ratio is determined by the base ratio.

3. Let h be the distance between $\overline{PQ}$ and $\overline{SR}$.

4. The base ratio equals the area ratio with fixed height. Use it to find the area of $\triangle SQR$.

2. In trapezoid $ABCD$ the lengths of the bases AB and CD are 8 and 17 respectively. The legs of the trapezoid are extended beyond A and B to meet at point E. Find the ratio of the area of triangle ECD to the area of trapezoid $ABCD$.

Walk-Through

1. Extend $\overline{AC}$ and $\overline{BD}$ to meet up at a point E.

2. If two triangles are similar with the length ratio $a : b$, then the area ratio equals $a^2 : b^2$.

3. Express the area of $\triangle EAB$ and $\triangle ECD$ with letter k.

4. Conclude solving the problem, manipulating the expressions with k.

3. Suppose that $PQRS$ is a trapezoid in which $\overline{PS}$ is parallel to $\overline{QR}$. If $\overline{PR}$ and $\overline{RS}$ form right angle, and $\overline{PR}$ bisects angle $\angle SPQ$, and $[PQRS] = 144$, then compute $[\triangle PQR]$.

Walk-Through

1. Find T on $\overline{SP}$ such that $ST = TP$.

2. Find an associated rhombus $PTRQ$.

3. Find the area $[PQR]$ using $[PTR]$ and $[STR]$.

4. Out of the inner region of the following isosceles trapezoid, the region closer to the top base relative to other sides has the area of $A\sqrt{3}$. Find the value of A.

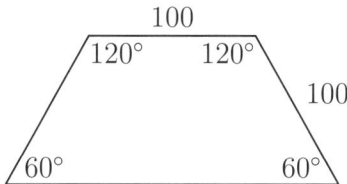

> **Walk-Through**
>
> 1. Draw angle bisectors of the top corner angles.
>
> 2. Color the region closer to the top base.
>
> 3. Draw the midsegment and color the upper region.
>
> 4. Find the area of trapezoid A.

5. What is the area of a rhombus with side length $\sqrt{149}$ units and diagonals that differ by 6 units?

Walk-Through

1. Draw a rhombus by sketching two perpendicular bisectors.

2. Label half of diagonals with a letter k.

3. Set up a Pythagorean Theorem.

4. The area of rhombus is half the product of diagonals.

6. In trapezoid $ABCD$, $\overline{AB}$ is parallel to $\overline{CD}$, $AB = 7$ units, and $CD = 10$ units. Segment $\overline{EF}$ is drawn parallel to $\overline{AB}$ with E lying on $\overline{AD}$ and F lying on $\overline{BC}$ such that $BF : FC = 5 : 7$. Let G be the point on $\overline{EF}$ such that it is the point of intersection between $\overline{EF}$ and $\overline{BD}$. If $|EG - GF| = \dfrac{p}{q}$ where p and q are relatively prime, find $p + q$.

Walk-Through

1. Find the ratio $GF : DC$.

2. Evaluate the exact value of GF.

3. Find the ratio $GE : AB$.

4. Evaluate the exact value of GE.

5. Determine $|EG - GF|$ using FG and EG.

7. In trapezoid $PQRS$, $\overline{PQ}$ and $\overline{RS}$ are perpendicular to $\overline{PS}$, with $PQ + 2RS = QR$, $PS = 9$, with PQ and RS distinct integers, what is the length of $\overline{QR}$?

> **Walk-Through**
>
> 1. Label PQ and RS as x and y, respectively.
>
> 2. Find QR in terms of x and y.
>
> 3. Set up a Pythagorean Theorem.
>
> 4. Solve for quadratic equation, and find (x, y).
>
> 5. There is only one unique pair (x, y). Hence, find QR.

8. In a trapezoid $ABCD$ with AB parallel to CD, the diagonals AC and BD intersect at E. If the area of triangle ABE is 35 square units, and the area of triangle ADE is 15 square units, what is the area of trapezoid $ABCD$?

Walk-Through

1. Find $[BCE]$. Hence, find the length ratio between DE and BE.

2. Find the area ratio between $[DCE]$ and $[BAE]$.

3. Hence, find $[DCE]$.

4. Find the area of trapezoid $ABCD$.

9. If an obtuse isosceles triangle is inscribed in a circle with radius $10\sqrt{2}$, where the two sides of equal length have the measure of 10, what is the length of its base?

> **Walk-Through**
>
> 1. Let θ be the base angle.
>
> 2. Then, notice that the central angle of a chord is 2θ.
>
> 3. Find $\cos(\theta)$ by dropping a perpendicular bisector of the vertex angle to the base.
>
> 4. Use $\cos(\theta)$ to find the length of the base.
>
> 5. Unlike the walk-through, the solution manual describes how to use the law of cosines.

10. Given a quadrilateral $ABCD$ where $\angle ABC = \angle ACD = 90°$, $AC = 12$, and $CD = 18$, two diagonals $\overline{AC}$ and $\overline{BD}$ intersect at point E such that E is the midpoint of $\overline{AC}$. Let F be the perpendicular foot from B to AC. Find the length of EF.

Walk-Through

1. Label EF with a letter x.

2. Set up a Pythagorean Theorem with AB, BC, and AC.

3. Solve for x, and conclude solving the problem.

4. On the other hand, one may use similar right triangles to find the value of x.

11. Given a right isosceles triangle ABC where B is the right angle, and $AB = BC = 4$. Let D be the midpoint of $\overline{AC}$, M a point on $\overline{BC}$ and N on $\overline{BA}$ such that $BM > BN$. If a quadrilateral $BMDN$ is cyclic and $MN = 3$, find the area of MDN.

Walk-Through

1. Use a cyclic $BMDN$, perform angle-chasing to figure out inscribed angles.

2. Classify a triangle MDN.

3. Find ND and MD.

4. Find the area of MDN.

12. In quadrilateral $ABCD$, $BC = 4$, $CD = 5$, and $DA = 6$ and $m\angle A = m\angle B = 60°$, find the area of $ABCD$.

> **Walk-Through**
>
> 1. Find the height from D to $\overline{AB}$.
>
> 2. Find the height from C to $\overline{AB}$.
>
> 3. Find the lower base length.
>
> 4. Add two right-triangles and a trapezoid to find the area of $ABCD$.

13. Convex quadrilateral $ABCD$ with $AB = 4$ and $CD = 5$ has diagonals AC and BD intersected at E, and $\triangle AED$ and $\triangle BEC$ have equal areas. Find the ratio of $[ABE] : [CDE]$.

Walk-Through

1. Interpret the meaning of $[AED] = [BEC]$.

2. Use $AB : CD$ to find out the area of $[ABE] : [CDE]$.

3. Step 1 is the key idea of understanding the nature of special convex quadrilateral the problem proposes.

14. Suppose that P is a point on minor arc BC of the circumcircle of equilateral triangle ABC. If $PB = 4$, $PC = 6$, then find the length of $\overline{PA}$.

> **Walk-Through**
>
> 1. Apply Ptolemy's Formula on the cyclic quadrilateral $PBCA$.
>
> 2. Let k be the side length of equilateral triangle ABC.
>
> 3. According to Ptolemy, $PA \cdot BC = PB \cdot AC + PC \cdot AB$. Hence, find the length PA.

15. Triangle $\triangle ABC$ has a right angle at C, $\angle A = 45°$, and $AC = 10$. Find the radius of the incircle of $\triangle ABC$.

> **Walk-Through**
>
> 1. Let r be the inradius of $\triangle ABC$.
>
> 2. Perform length-chasing to find out AB in terms of r.
>
> 3. Solve for r, and conclude solving the problem.

16. A quarter circle centered at O, with the radius of 16, has a semicircle inside it whose diameter is the radius of the quarter circle. If there is another semicircle inside the quarter circle such that it is externally tangent to the semicircle previously mentioned and its diameter is on the other side of the quarter circle, find the radius of the smaller semicircle.

Walk-Through

1. Let x be the radius of the smaller semicircle.

2. Externally tangent condition produces an equation using Pythagorean Theorem.

3. Apply Pythagorean Theorem with respect to x, and find the length of x.

17. If a regular octagon with the side length of 200 is inscribed in a circle with diameter of length d, then $\dfrac{d^2}{40000}$ can be written as $a + b\sqrt{c}$ where a, b, and c are positive integers and c is not divisible by the square of any prime. Find $a+b+c$.

> **Walk-Through**
>
> 1. Regular octagon consists of numerous right isosceles triangles.
> 2. Set up an equation using Pythagorean Theorem.
> 3. Expand the expression to find out $\dfrac{d^2}{40000}$.
> 4. Hence, find $a+b+c$ from $a+b\sqrt{c}$.

18. Let $\triangle ABC$ be a right triangle such that B is a right angle. Circles with diameter of AB and of BC meet at a point D other than B. If $AD = 6$ and $BD = 4$, then find the length of $\overline{CD}$.

> **Walk-Through**
>
> 1. Recall that circumdiameter equals hypotenuse, given a right triangle.
>
> 2. In particular, classify a triangle ABD and BCD.
>
> 3. Label the angle A as θ. Find the measure of $m\angle CBD$.
>
> 4. Use similarity to find the length CD.

19. Three circles with radii 2, 3, and 4 are externally tangent to each other. Find the area of triangle formed by connecting the centers.

> **Walk-Through**
>
> 1. Connect all centers to find the triangle.
>
> 2. Label all of their sides with specific lengths.
>
> 3. Use Heron's formula to find out the area of triangle. In particular, the area of a triangle with side lengths a, b, and c, equals $\sqrt{s(s-a)(s-b)(s-c)}$ where $s = \dfrac{a+b+c}{2}$.

20. In circle centered at P, $\overline{AB}$ is perpendicular to $\overline{CD}$ at X. If $AX = 3$, $BX = 8$, $CX = 6$ and $DX = 4$, then find the radius of the circle.

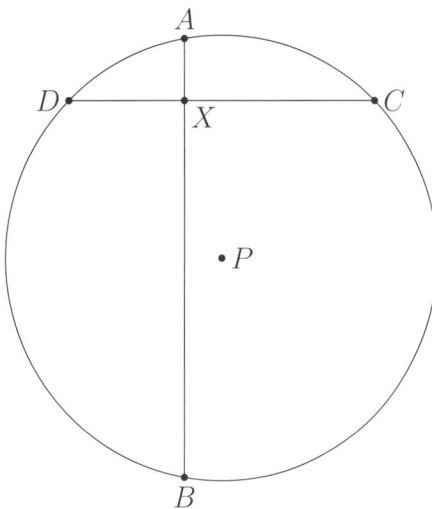

Walk-Through

1. The perpendicular bisector of a chord always passes through the circle's center.

2. Draw perpendicular bisectors of $\overline{AB}$ and $\overline{CD}$.

3. Set up Pythagorean Theorem to find the radius of a circle.

4. Let r be its radius.

5. Find half of $\overline{AB}$.

6. Find the distance from P to $\overline{AB}$.

7. Use Pythagorean Theorem to find r.

Answer Key

1. 16

Draw an auxiliary line passing through Q such that it is parallel to $\overline{PS}$. Let the intersection point between the auxiliary line and $\overline{PS}$ be T. Then, $\triangle PQS$, $\triangle QST$, and $\triangle QRT$ all have the same area since the base lengths are equal to one another. Hence, $\triangle SQR$ has the area of 16.

2. $\dfrac{289}{225}$

Extend $\overline{CA}$ and $\overline{BD}$ to meet up at a point E. Then, $\triangle EAB$ and $\triangle ECD$ are similar with the length ratio of 8 to 17. Hence, the area ratio between $\triangle ECD$ and $\square ABCD$ is $17^2 : 17^2 - 8^2$. Hence, the answer is $289 : 225 = \dfrac{289}{225}$.

3. 48

Let T be the point on $\overline{SP}$ such that $ST = TP$. Then, $PT = TR = RQ = QP$, which matches with the definition of a rhombus. Hence, $[PQR] = [PTR] = [STR]$, so $[PQR] = 144/3 = 48$.

4. 1875

Draw angle bisectors and midsegment for proper regions. Since the midsegment has the length of 150, then we get the lower base of length of 50 for the smaller trapezoid. Since its height is half the original figure, we get the area of $\dfrac{1}{2}(50+100)(25\sqrt{3}) = 1875\sqrt{3}$. Therefore, the answer must be 1875.

5. 140

Let a and $a+3$ be half the length of each diagonal. Then, $a^2 + (a+3)^2 = 149$. Hence, $2a^2 + 6a + 9 = 149$. Therefore, $a^2 + 3a - 70 = (a-7)(a+10) = 0$. Thus, $a = 7$. The area of rhombus is $7 \times 10 \times 2 = 140$.

6. 13

First, $GF : DC = 5 : 12$, by given information. Hence, $GF = 50/12$. Likewise, $GE : AB = 7 : 12$, so $GE = 49/12$. Thus, $|EG - GF| = GF - GE = 1/12$. Since 1 and 12 are relatively prime, $p + q = 1 + 12 = 13$.

7. 15

Let $PQ = x$ and $SR = y$, then $QR = x + 2y$. Therefore, by Pythagorean theorem, $(x+2y)^2 = 9^2 + (y-x)^2$, so $81 = 3y(y + 2x)$. Hence, $27 = y(y+2x)$, so $(y, y+2x) = (27, 1), (9, 3), (3, 9)$ and $(1, 27)$. Since $x \neq y$, $(y, x) = (1, 13)$. Thus, $QR = 13 + 2(1) = 15$.

8. $\dfrac{500}{7}$

Since $[ADE] = 15$, we also get $[BCE] = 15$. Thus, $DE : BE = 3 : 7$. Since the length ratio is $3 : 7$, the area ratio between two similar triangles DCE and BAE is $9 : 49$. Hence, $[DCE] = 45/7$. Thus, the area of the trapezoid is $500/7 (= 15 + 15 + 45/7 + 35)$.

9. $5\sqrt{14}$

Let the central angle for the chord of length 10 be θ. Then, the law of cosines states that $100 = 400 - 400\cos(\theta)$. Hence, $\cos(\theta) = 3/4$. Hence,
$\cos(2\theta) = 2\cos^2(\theta) - 1 = 2(3/4)^2 - 1 = 1/8$.
Therefore, $x^2 = 400 - 400(1/8) = 350$.
Thus, $x = \sqrt{350} = 5\sqrt{14}$.

10. $\dfrac{3\sqrt{10}}{5}$

Let EF be x. Then, by Pythagoras Theorem, $AB^2 + BC^2 = AC^2$. Hence, $(6-x)^2 + (3x)^2 + (6+x)^2 + (3x)^2 = 144$. Thus, $20x^2 = 72$. Hence, $x = 3\sqrt{10}/5$.

OR

Use similar right triangles to solve $(3x)^2 = (6-x)(6+x)$. Hence, $9x^2 = 36 - x^2$, so $10x^2 = 36$. Therefore, $x^2 = 36/10$, so $x = \sqrt{36/10} = 6\sqrt{10}/10 = 3\sqrt{10}/5$.

11. $\dfrac{9}{4}$

Notice that MDN is a right isosceles triangle since $\angle CBD \cong \angle MND$ and $\angle NBD \cong \angle NMD$. Hence, $MN = 3$ implies that $ND = MD = \dfrac{3}{\sqrt{2}}$. Therefore, the area of this triangle is
$\dfrac{1}{2} \cdot \dfrac{3}{\sqrt{2}} \cdot \dfrac{3}{\sqrt{2}} = \dfrac{9}{4}$.

12. $\dfrac{5\sqrt{66} + 13\sqrt{3}}{2}$

The height from D to $\overline{AB}$ is $3\sqrt{3}$ and that from C to $\overline{AB}$ is $2\sqrt{3}$. Using $30 - 60 - 90$ right triangle, we get the lower base length of $3 + \sqrt{22} + 2 = 5 + \sqrt{22}$. However, we cut the region into three parts - two right triangles and one trapezoid. Hence, we get the area of

$$\dfrac{1}{2}(9\sqrt{3} + 4\sqrt{3}) + \dfrac{1}{2}(3\sqrt{3} + 2\sqrt{3})(\sqrt{22})$$

Hence, the area is $\dfrac{5\sqrt{66} + 13\sqrt{3}}{2}$.

13. $\dfrac{16}{25}$

$\triangle AED$ and $\triangle BEC$ have equal areas, meaning that $ABCD$ is trapezoid. Hence, $AB : CD = 4 : 5$ implies that the area ratio must be $16 : 25$.

14. 10

Let r be the length of equilateral triangle. By Ptolemy, $6r + 4r = PA \cdot r$. Hence, $PA = 10$.

15. $10 - 5\sqrt{2}$

Let r be the radius of incircle. Then, $2(10 - r) = 10\sqrt{2}$, by chasing lengths. Hence, $r = 10 - 5\sqrt{2}$.

16. $\dfrac{16}{3}$

Let x be the radius of the smaller semicircle. Since two semicircles are externally tangent to each other, we get $8^2 + (16-x)^2 = (8+x)^2$. Hence, $x = \dfrac{16}{3}$.

17. 8

Using Pythagoras theorem and properties of isosceles trapezoid, we get

$$d^2 = (200)^2 + (200 + 200\sqrt{2})^2$$

Hence, $d^2/40000 = 1 + (1+\sqrt{2})^2$. Therefore,

$$1 + 1 + 2\sqrt{2} + 2 = 4 + 2\sqrt{2}$$
$$= a + b\sqrt{c}$$

Thus, $a + b + c = 4 + 2 + 2 = 8$.

18. $\dfrac{8}{3}$

By similarity, we get $AD : BD = BD : CD$. Let $CD = x$. Then, $6 \cdot x = 4^2$. Hence, $x = \dfrac{8}{3}$.

19. $6\sqrt{6}$

First, the triangle connecting three centers has the side lengths 5, 6, and 7. Since all side lengths are integers, use Heron's Formula. Since $s = \dfrac{5+6+7}{2} = 9$, the area must be

$$\sqrt{9(9-5)(9-6)(9-7)} = 6\sqrt{6}$$

20. $\dfrac{5\sqrt{5}}{2}$

Let $PB = PC = r$. Notice that the perpendicular bisector of $\overline{CD}$ passes through P. Likewise, the perpendicular bisector of $\overline{AB}$ passes through P as well. Hence, using Pythagoras theorem on a right triangle formed by connecting one of the perpendicular bisector to P with the radius, we get

$$r^2 = (\dfrac{11}{2})^2 + 1^2$$
$$= (\dfrac{5}{2})^2 + 5^2$$
$$= \dfrac{125}{4}$$

Hence, $r = \dfrac{5\sqrt{5}}{2}$.

TOPIC 8

More About Algebra 2 / Precalculus

8.1 About Polynomials

8.2 Maximum and Minimum

8.3 Floor Function

8.4 Sequence and Series

8.5 Using Trigonometry for Angle Equations

8.6 Complex Plane Geometry and Vectors

8.7 Practices

8.1 About Polynomials

When we talk about polynomials in high-school competition, we usually talk about Viete's formula, Newton's identity, polynomial interpolations, and algebraic manipulations. Let's delve into each theme one at a time.

First, given a polynomial $p(x) = a_n x^n + a_{n-1} x^{n-1} + a_{n-2} x^{n-2} + \cdots + a_1 x + a_0$, and let r_i be its roots for $i = 1, 2, 3, \cdots, n$. Then, Viete's formula states that

- $r_1 + r_2 + \cdots + r_n = -\dfrac{a_{n-1}}{a_n}$.

- $r_1 r_2 + r_1 r_3 + \cdots + r_{n-1} r_n = \dfrac{a_{n-2}}{a_n}$.

- $\vdots$

- $r_1 r_2 r_3 \cdots r_n = (-1)^n \dfrac{a_0}{a_n}$.

Example Given a cubic equation $x^3 - 4x^2 + 5x - 1 = 0$, let r, s, and t be solutions. Find $r + s + t$.

Solution First, write $x^3 - 4x^2 + 5x - 1 = (x-r)(x-s)(x-t)$. Then, expand the right-side to find that $-(r + s + t) = -4$. Hence, we conclude that $r + s + t = 4$.

Now, extending Viete's formula a bit further, we get Newton's identity, which oftentimes appears in recent math competitions. Consider a polynomial $a_n x^n + a_{n-1} x^{n-1} + \cdots + a_1 + a_0$, with n roots, which we'll denote as $\{x_1, x_2, \cdots, x_n\}$. Let's define the power of roots as

$$S_k = x_1^k + x_2^k + \ldots + x_n^k$$

for $k = 1, 2, \ldots, n$. In particular, $S_1 = x_1 + x_2 + \cdots + x_n$. Then, the following properties hold true.

1. $a_n S_1 + a_{n-1} = 0$. (Note that this is a direct application of Viete's formula.)

2. $a_n S_2 + a_{n-1} S_1 + a_{n-2}(2) = 0$.

3. $a_n S_3 + a_{n-1} S_2 + a_{n-2} S_1 + a_{n-3}(3) = 0$.

4. $\vdots$

These identities can be extended to higher degrees as well. Now, the following example will provide you with specific details and illustrate how Newton's identity is deduced.

Example Given a cubic equation $x^3 - 4x^2 + 5x - 1 = 0$, let r, s, and t be solutions. Find $r^3 + s^3 + t^3$.

Solution This example will directly show how Newton would have found this identity. Let $S_1 = r + s + t$, $S_2 = r^2 + s^2 + t^2$, and $S_3 = r^3 + s^3 + t^3$.

According to Newton's identity, we get $S_1 = 4$, $S_2 - 4S_1 + 5(2) = 0$, and $S_3 - 4S_2 + 5S_1 - 1(3) = 0$. We can recursively find out that $S_1 = 4$, $S_2 = 6$, and $S_3 = 7$.

On the other hand, we simply plug r, s, and t to find out $r^3 + s^3 + t^3$. In other words,

$$r^3 - 4r^2 + 5r - 1 = 0$$
$$s^3 - 4s^2 + 5s - 1 = 0$$
$$t^3 - 4t^2 + 5t - 1 = 0$$

Vertically summing up these three equations at the same time, we get $S_3 - 4S_2 + 5S - 1(3) = 0$. Now, one may understand how to deduce Newton's identity.

Third sub-topic to cover in this polynomial section is *polynomial interpolation*. This has something to do with "identity theorem." Here is one easy way to think about identity theorem. If there are two linear functions $f(x) = mx + b$ and $g(x) = px + q$ for some real m, b, p and q, if $f(x) = g(x)$ holds true for more than one real value of x, we say $f(x)$ and $g(x)$ are *identical* and conclude that $m = p$ and $b = q$.

Example Given a polynomial function $p(x) = x^4 + ax^2 + bx + c$, if $p(x) = x - 1$ for $x = 1, 2$, and 3, find c.

Solution Let $Q(x) = p(x) - x + 1$. Then, $Q(1) = Q(2) = Q(3) = 0$. Since $p(x) - x + 1$ is a 4th degree polynomial, then we can write $Q(x) = (x-1)(x-2)(x-3)(x-r)$ for some r.

Victe's formula implies that $r - -6$, since the sum of roots equals 0. Therefore, $Q(x) = (x-1)(x-2)(x-3)(x+6) = x^4 + ax^2 + (b-1)x + (c+1)$. Hence, $c + 1 = -36$. Therefore, $c = -37$.

Lastly, the followings are some algebraic formula, normally appearing in Algebra 2, which appears in high-school math competitions.

- $a^2 + b^2 = (a+b)^2 - 2ab = (a-b)^2 + 2ab$.

- $a^2 + b^2 + c^2 = (a+b+c)^2 - 2(ab+bc+ac)$.

- $a^3 + b^3 + c^3 - 3abc = (a+b+c)(a^2+b^2+c^2-ab-bc-ca) = \frac{1}{2}(a+b+c)((a-b)^2 + (b-c)^2 + (c-a)^2)$

- $a^4 + 4b^4 = (a^4 + 4a^2b^2 + 4b^4) - (4a^2b^2) = (a^2 - 2ab + 2b^2)(a^2 + 2ab + 2b^2)$. This is known as the Sophie-Germain Identity.

8.2 Maximum and Minimum

There are three main max/min set-ups we can use in competition math - trivial, AM-GM, and Cauchy-Schwarz inequality.

1. Given a real x, then $x^2 \geq 0$. This is known as trivial inequality, and completing the square lets us find minimum or maximum values.

2. Given non-negative real $x_1, x_2, \cdots, x_k$, then their arithmetic mean is at least their geometric mean, i.e., $\dfrac{x_1 + x_2 + \cdots + x_k}{k} \geq \sqrt[k]{x_1 x_2 \cdots x_k}$. This is well-used with polynomial over polynomial form.

3. For any list of reals $a_1, a_2, \cdots, a_n$ and $b_1, b_2, \cdots, b_n$, Cauchy-Schwarz inequality states that

$$(a_1^2 + a_2^2 + \cdots + a_n^2)(b_1^2 + b_2^2 + \cdots + b_n^2) \geq (a_1 b_1 + a_2 b_2 + \cdots + a_n b_n)^2,$$

with equality holding if and only if there exists a constant k such that $a_i = k b_i$ for all $1 \leq i \leq n$, or if one list consists of only zeroes.

Example For positive real x, determine the minimum value of $\dfrac{x^2 + 4}{x}$.

Solution For positive real x, $\dfrac{x^2 + 4}{x} = x + \dfrac{4}{x} \geq 2\sqrt{x \cdot \dfrac{4}{x}} = 2\sqrt{4} = 4$. The equality holds true if $x = \dfrac{4}{x}$. In other words, if $x = 2$, then the minimum value of $\dfrac{4 + 4}{2} = 4$ will be reached.

Example For real r, s, and t, satisfying $r^2 + s^2 + t^2 = 14$, determine the maximum possible value of $r + 2s + 3t$.

Solution According to Cauchy-Schwarz inequality,

$$(1r + 2s + 3t)^2 \leq (1^2 + 2^2 + 3^2)(r^2 + s^2 + t^2) = 14^2$$

Hence, $r + 2s + 3t \leq 14$. We must check whether the equality holds true. Let $\dfrac{r}{1} = \dfrac{s}{2} = \dfrac{t}{3} = k$ for some k. Then, $r = k$, $s = 2k$, and $t = 3k$. Since $k^2 + 4k^2 + 9k^2 = 14k^2 = 14$, we get $k = \pm 1$. Since we are looking for maximum possible value, let $k = 1$. Then,

$$r + 2s + 3t = 1 + 2(2) + 3(3) = 1 + 4 + 9 = 14.$$

8.3 Floor Function

Floor function $y = \lfloor x \rfloor$, for real x, is defined as the greatest integer less than or equal to x. For instance, $\lfloor 1.23 \rfloor = 1$. Likewise, $\lfloor -1.23 \rfloor = -2$.

The difference between x and $\lfloor x \rfloor$ is the decimal part of x, denoted by $\{x\}$. This is always between 0 and 1. When floor function appears in competition math, we must utilize two sets of strategies.

1. Algebra : Perform casework on integer intervals of x, or use the boundedness of $\{x\}$.

2. Graph : Sketch the graph of a floor function by cutting the original function sitting inside the floor symbol in integer intervals of y.

Example Determine the number of real solutions for
$\{\log_2(x)\} = \log_2(x) - \lfloor \log_2(x) \rfloor = \dfrac{1}{2}$ for $1 < x < 1024$.
Solution Graphing $\{\log_2(x)\}$, we notice that there are graph portions between $1 \leq x < 2, 2 \leq x < 4, 4 \leq x < 8, \cdots$, and $512 \leq x < 1024$. Each graph portion intersects $y = \dfrac{1}{2}$ exactly once. Hence, there are 10 intersections between $y = \{\log_2(x)\}$ and $y = \dfrac{1}{2}$.

Example Find the area of the region satisfying $\lfloor x \rfloor^2 + \lfloor y \rfloor^2 = 10$ for real x and y.
Solution Refer to the following graph, where each colored grid shows the solution to the given equation. Notice that $(\lfloor x \rfloor, \lfloor y \rfloor) = (\pm 1, \pm 3), (\pm 3, \pm 1), (\mp 1, \pm 3)$, and $(\mp 3, \pm 1)$, whose graphs can be drawn in the following xy-plane.

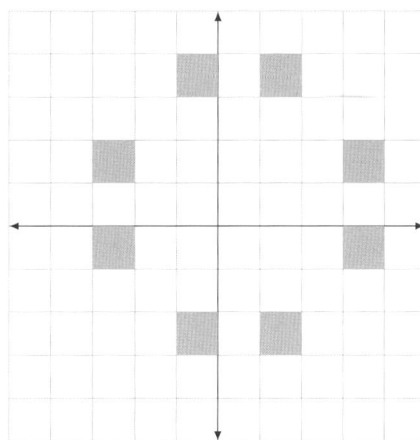

As one can see from the graph, gray regions are the solutions to the given equation. Hence, the area of the region equals 8.

8.4 Sequence and Series

The most fundamental idea about sequence is that we use 1-to-1 correspondence. Arithmetic sequence is basically a linear function, and geometric sequence is an exponential function, both of which are one-to-one functions.

1. Arithmetic sequence : $a_n = a_1 + (n-1)d$ where a_1 is the first term and d is the common difference.

2. Geometric sequence : $b_n = b_1 r^{n-1}$ where b_1 is the first term and r is the common ratio.

Example If $p(x) = x^3 - 3x^2 + ax + b$ has its roots forming an arithmetic sequence, determine the value of $a + b$.

Solution Let r, s, and t be roots. Without loss of generality, assume that $r \leq s \leq t$. Then, $r = s - d$ and $t = s + d$ for some common difference d. Then, $r + s + t = 3s = 3$ by Viete's formula. This implies that $p(1) = 1^3 - 3(1^2) + a(1) + b = 0$. Hence, $a + b = 2$.

The sum of sequential terms is known as series, and we use the sigma notation for summation, i.e.,

$$\sum_{k=1}^{n} a_k = a_1 + a_2 + a_3 + \cdots + a_n = S_n$$

The following three formulas are mostly used in competition math, but in the practices, we will see one example to deduce the sum of fourth powers, using combinatorial approach.

- $1 + 2 + 3 + \cdots + n = \dfrac{n(n+1)}{2}$.

- $1^2 + 2^2 + \cdots + n^2 = \dfrac{n(n+1)(2n+1)}{6}$.

- $1^3 + 2^3 + \cdots + n^3 = \left(\dfrac{n(n+1)}{2}\right)^2$.

Other than the above formula, one may encounter telescoping series, which normally cancels out terms when added. Read the following example carefully.

Example Rewrite the following summation into a reduced fraction.

$$\sum_{k=1}^{10} \frac{k!}{(k+2)!}$$

Solution

$$\sum_{k=1}^{10} \frac{k!}{(k+2)!} = \sum_{k=1}^{10} \frac{1}{(k+1)(k+2)} = \sum_{k=1}^{10} \frac{1}{k+1} - \frac{1}{k+2} = \left(\frac{1}{2} - \frac{1}{3}\right) + \cdots + \left(\frac{1}{11} - \frac{1}{12}\right) = \frac{5}{12}$$

8.5 Using Trigonometry for Angle Equations

In this section, we study how "angle" can be used as a variable, and how trigonometry helps solve a geometry problem. We simply put a set of identities commonly used in competition math. Refer to the appendix for basic trigonometry.

- Given a right triangle, side lengths can be interconnected, as shown in the following figure.

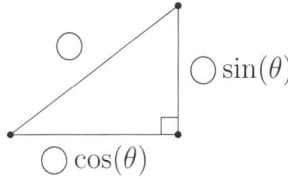

- $\cos(\theta) = \sin(90° - \theta)$; $\sin(\theta) = \sin(180° - \theta)$; $\cos(\theta) = -\cos(180° - \theta)$.

- $\cos(a \pm b) = \cos(a)\cos(b) \mp \sin(a)\sin(b)$; $\sin(a \pm b) = \sin(a)\cos(b) \pm \cos(a)\sin(b)$.

- $\tan(a \pm b) = \dfrac{\tan(a) \pm \tan(b)}{1 \mp \tan(a)\tan(b)}$.

Example In the following diagram, determine the value of $\sin(EAF)$, where E and F are the midpoints of the sides on which they stay.

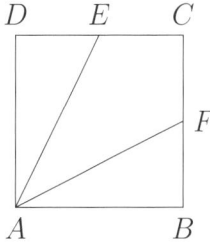

Solution

1. Label θ as $m\angle EAF$ and α as $m\angle EAD = m\angle FAB$.
2. Notice that $\theta + 2\alpha = 90°$.
3. $\sin(\theta) = \sin(90° - 2\alpha) = \cos(2\alpha) = \cos^2(\alpha) - \sin^2(\alpha)$.
4. Let $DE = BF = k$. Then, $AD = AB = 2k$, so $AE = AF = \sqrt{5}k$.
5. Hence, $\cos(\alpha) = \dfrac{2k}{\sqrt{5}k}$ and $\sin(\alpha) = \dfrac{k}{\sqrt{5}k}$.
6. Thus,

$$\sin(\theta) = \cos^2(\alpha) - \sin^2(\alpha)$$
$$= \frac{4}{5} - \frac{1}{5}$$
$$= \frac{4-1}{5}$$
$$= \frac{3}{5}$$

8.6 Complex Plane Geometry and Vectors

Here are the tools we use for complex plane geometry.

1. A rectangular coordinate (x, y) can be re-expressed as $x = r\cos(\theta)$ and $y = r\sin(\theta)$ where $r = \sqrt{x^2 + y^2}$ and $\theta = \arctan\left(\dfrac{y}{x}\right)$.

2. $z = a + bi = r(\cos(\theta) + i\sin(\theta)) = re^{i\theta}$.

3. $\cos(\theta) = \dfrac{z + \overline{z}}{2}$ and $\sin(\theta) = \dfrac{z - \overline{z}}{2i}$.

4. For complex numbers, triangular inequality holds true. For complex u and v, assuming that $|u| \geq |v|$, then $|u| - |v| \leq |u + v| \leq |u| + |v|$. (Refer to problem 30.)

Example Find the complex number z such that $|z - 2| = |z + 1| = |z - 2i|$.

Solution

\# 1. Let $z = a + bi$ for real a and b.

\# 2. Then, $|z - 2| = |(a - 2) + bi| = \sqrt{(a - 2)^2 + b^2}$;
$|z + 1| = |(a + 1) + bi| = \sqrt{(a + 1)^2 + b^2}$; $|z - 2i| = |a + (b - 2)i| = \sqrt{a^2 + (b - 2)^2}$.

\# 3. This is equivalent to finding the point of concurrency from $(-1, 0)$, $(2, 0)$ and $(0, 2)$.

\# 4. The perpendicular bisector of $(-1, 0)$ and $(2, 0)$ is $x = \dfrac{1}{2}$. Likewise, the perpendicular bisector of $(2, 0)$ and $(0, 2)$ is $y = x$.

\# 5. Hence, the point of concurrency is $\left(\dfrac{1}{2}, \dfrac{1}{2}\right)$. Thus, $z = \dfrac{1}{2} + \dfrac{i}{2}$.

Example Evaluate

$$\tan 5° \times \tan 25° \times \tan 45° \times \cdots \times \tan 165°.$$

Solution

\# 1. Notice that

$$\tan n\theta = \frac{\sin n\theta}{\cos n\theta}$$

$$= \frac{\binom{n}{1}\cos^{n-1}\theta \sin\theta - \binom{n}{3}\cos^{n-3}\theta \sin^3\theta + \binom{n}{5}\cos^{n-5}\theta \sin^5\theta - \cdots}{\cos^n\theta - \binom{n}{2}\cos^{n-2}\theta \sin^2\theta + \binom{n}{4}\cos^{n-4}\theta \sin^4\theta - \cdots}$$

$$= \frac{\binom{n}{1}\tan\theta - \binom{n}{3}\tan^3\theta + \binom{n}{5}\tan^5\theta - \cdots}{1 - \binom{n}{2}\tan^2\theta + \binom{n}{4}\tan^4\theta - \cdots}.$$

\# 2. If $n = 9$, then $\tan 9\theta = \dfrac{9\tan\theta - 84\tan^3\theta + 126\tan^5\theta - 36\tan^7\theta + \tan^9\theta}{1 - 36\tan^2\theta + 126\tan^4\theta - 84\tan^6\theta + 9\tan^8\theta}$.

3. Let $t = \tan\theta$, so $1 = \dfrac{9t - 84t^3 + 126t^5 - 36t^7 + t^9}{1 - 36t^2 + 126t^4 - 84t^6 + 9t^8}$.

4. It is easy to check that $\tan(5°), \tan(25°), \cdots, \tan(165°)$ are roots of

$$t^9 - 9t^8 - 36t^7 + 84t^6 + 126t^5 - 126t^4 - 84t^3 + 36t^2 + 9t - 1 = 0.$$

5. By Viete's formula, their product is 1.

Vector is an object with both magnitude and direction. If we write it $<a, b>$, then it represents an arrow that starts from $(0, 0)$ and ends at (a, b).

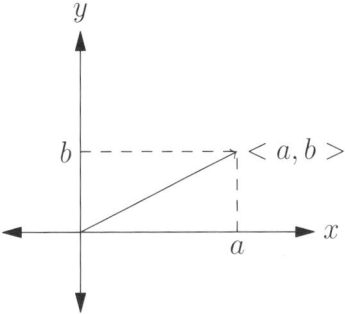

If the length of the vector is $r = \sqrt{a^2 + b^2}$, and the angle θ formed by the vector and the x-axis satisfies $\tan(\theta) = \dfrac{b}{a}$, then

$$<a, b> = <r\cos(\theta), r\sin(\theta)>$$

It is not difficult to check that (a, b) can be interpreted as $<a, b>$, $<r\cos(\theta), r\sin(\theta)>$, $r(\cos(\theta) + i\sin(\theta))$, or $re^{i\theta}$.

The following applications of vectors could help some challenging problems in competition math.

1. Vector questions are directly connected to the laws of cosines, i.e.,

$$|\mathbf{r} + \mathbf{s}|^2 = |\mathbf{r}|^2 + |\mathbf{s}|^2 - 2|\mathbf{r}||\mathbf{s}|\cos(\alpha)$$

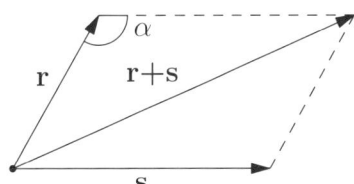

2. Let $\vec{v} = <a, b>$ and $\vec{u} = <c, d>$. The area of associated triangle formed by $(0, 0)$, (a, b) and (c, d) can be found by half the absolute value of determinant $\begin{vmatrix} a & b \\ c & d \end{vmatrix} = ad - bc$. This is also a direct application of shoelace theorem.

Example Find the area of a triangle whose coordinates are $(1,1)$, $(2,5)$ and $(6,3)$.

Solution

1. We may apply shoelace theorem, i.e.,
$$\frac{1}{2}|(1(5) + 2(3) + 6(1)) - (1(2) + 5(6) + 3(1))| = \frac{1}{2}(18) = 9.$$

2. Or, let $\vec{u} = <2,5> - <1,1> = <1,4>$ and $\vec{v} = <6,3> - <1,1> = <5,2>$. The area must be $\frac{1}{2}\begin{vmatrix} 1 & 4 \\ 5 & 2 \end{vmatrix} = \frac{1}{2}|2 - 20| = 9.$

8.7 Practices

1. For a natural number n, if $x^2 - nx + 2n = 0$ has rational roots, compute the sum of all possible values of n.

> **Walk-Through**
>
> 1. When a quadratic equation has rational roots, it means that its discriminant must be a perfect square.
>
> 2. Set up $n^2 - 8n = k^2$ for some integer k.
>
> 3. Complete the square for n, and set up a difference of squares.
>
> 4. Find different values of n, and conclude solving the problem. Some values of n are repeated, so one must count them once.

2. The polynomial $x^4 - x^2 - 1 = 0$ has four roots $r_1, r_2, r_3,$ and r_4. Find the exact value of $(2+r_1)(2+r_2)(2+r_3)(2+r_4)$.

> **Walk-Through**
>
> 1. Viete's formula implies $x^4 - x^2 - 1 = (x-r_1)(x-r_2)(x-r_3)(x-r_4)$.
>
> 2. Notice that $(2+r_1)(2+r_2)(2+r_3)(2+r_4)$ can be changed into $(-2-r_1)(-2-r_2)(-2-r_3)(-2-r_4)$. Reason why it works.
>
> 3. Use step 1 to solve for step 2.

3. Let r, s, and t be complex numbers with r real, such that $r+s+t = rs+st+tr = 3$ and $rst = 10$. Then, r can be written as $\sqrt[a]{b}+c$ where b is a cube-free integer, a is a prime number, and c is a positive integer. Determine the sum of a, b, and c.

Walk-Through

1. Set up a cubic polynomial $(x-r)(x-s)(x-t) = 0$. Write it in expanded form.

2. Use $(a+b)^3 = a^3 + 3a^2b + 3ab^2 + b^3$ or $(a-b)^3 = a^3 - 3a^2b + 3ab^2 - b^3$. In particular, set $a = x$ and $b = 1$.

3. Turn the given cubic polynomial into a perfect cube.

4. Take a cube-root to both sides of the equation and solve for a, b, and c.

4. Let r, s, and t be solutions to $x^3 - 5x^2 + 6x - 1 = 0$. If the value of $\frac{1}{r} + \frac{1}{s} + \frac{1}{t}$ can be written as a positive integer k, determine the value of k.

Walk-Through

1. First, turn $\frac{1}{r} + \frac{1}{s} + \frac{1}{t}$ into a single fraction.

2. Use Viete's formula to find out $rs + st + tr$ and rst.

3. Second, let $p(x) = x^3 - 5x^2 + 6x - 1$. Find $p\left(\frac{1}{x}\right)$, and investigate its solutions.

4. Multiply $p\left(\frac{1}{x}\right)$ by x^3 to figure out a new polynomial whose solutions are listed in step 3.

5. Apply Viete's formula to find the sum of the roots in step 3.

5. Let r, s, and t be solutions to a cubic polynomial equation $x^3 - 5x^2 + 4x - 1 = 0$. Determine the value of $r^4 + s^4 + t^4$.

> **Walk-Through**
>
> 1. Apply Newton's identity.
>
> 2. Compute S_1 by $S_1 - 5(1) = 0$.
>
> 3. Compute S_2 by $S_2 - 5S_1 + 4(2) = 0$.
>
> 4. Compute S_3 by $S_3 - 5S_2 + 4S_1 - 1(3) = 0$.
>
> 5. Compute S_4 by $S_4 - 5S_3 + 4S_2 - S_1 = 0$.

6. Let r, s, and t be solutions to a cubic equation $x^3 - 5x^2 + 7x - 1 = 0$. If there exists a monic cubic polynomial $p(x)$ such that $p(r) = s + t$, $p(s) = r + t$, and $p(t) = r + s$, determine $p(1)$.

> **Walk-Through**
>
> 1. Use Viete's formula to find out $r + s + t$, $rs + st + tr$ and rst.
>
> 2. Rewrite $p(r) = s + t$, $p(s) = r + t$, and $p(t) = r + s$. In particular, use $r + s + t = 5$.
>
> 3. Find a monic cubic polynomial for $p(x) + x - 5$, a process of which is known as polynomial interpolation.
>
> 4. Substitute $x = 1$ into the expressions found in step 3, and conclude solving the problem.

7. Determine the smallest possible value of positive real k such that there exist real numbers r and s, not necessarily distinct, such that $r + s = rs = k$.

> **Walk-Through**
>
> 1. First, notice that r and s are positive real. Suppose otherwise and reach contradiction.
>
> 2. Apply AM-GM inequality for r and s. Find the smallest positive value of k.
>
> 3. Second, set up a monic quadratic equation $(x-r)(x-s) = 0$.
>
> 4. Set its discriminant greater than or equal to 0.
>
> 5. Solve for k, and compare the value found in step 2.

8. If $\dfrac{a+b}{c} + \dfrac{b+c}{a} + \dfrac{a+c}{b} = 1000$, then determine the exact value of

$$\dfrac{(a+b)(b+c)(a+c)}{abc}.$$

> **Walk-Through**
>
> 1. Turn $\dfrac{a+b}{c} + \dfrac{b+c}{a} + \dfrac{a+c}{b}$ into a single-denominator form.
>
> 2. Expand $(a+b)(b+c)(a+c)$.
>
> 3. Compare step 2 with step 1.
>
> 4. Substitute step 2 into the given fraction $\dfrac{(a+b)(b+c)(a+c)}{abc}$ and find the exact value.

262   The Essential Guide to **Competition Math**(Fundamentals Plus)

9. For integers a and b, determine the number of ordered pairs (a, b) satisfying $a^4 + 4b^4 = 1040$.

> **Walk-Through**
>
> 1. First, write down the first few perfect 4th powers, use $a^4 \geq 0$ and $b^4 \geq 0$.
>
> 2. Notice that there are few solution pairs satisfying the given equation.
>
> 3. Second, use Sophie-Germain identity to factorize $a^4 + 4b^4$ into the product of quadratics.
>
> 4. There is only one way of multiplying $a^2 + 2ab + 2b^2$ and $a^2 - 2ab + 2b^2$ to get the value of 1040.
>
> 5. Find the value of $a^2 + 2b^2$.
>
> 6. Find the unique pair (a^2, b^2) satisfying step 5.
>
> 7. Find all pairs (a, b) satisfying step 6.

10. If x, y and z are positive real solutions satisfying $x^2 + y^2 + z^2 = 110$ and $(x-y)^2 + (y-z)^2 + (z-x)^2 = 41$, determine the value of $x + y + z$.

> **Walk-Through**
>
> 1. Expand $(x-y)^2 + (y-z)^2 + (z-x)^2$.
>
> 2. Find $xy + yz + zx$.
>
> 3. Notice that $(a+b+c)^2 = a^2 + b^2 + c^2 + 2(ab+bc+ca)$.
>
> 4. Recall that x, y, and z are positive real numbers. Find the exact value of $x + y + z$.

11. Determine the largest possible volume of parallelepiped *inscribed* in the xy-plane, xz-plane, yz-plane and the plane $x + y + z = 12$. (For simplicity, assume that the parallelepiped must have three of its faces on the xy-plane, xz-plane, yz-plane.

Walk-Through

1. Draw a parallelepiped according to the condition.

2. Set up its volume in terms of x, y and z.

3. Use AM-GM inequality for three-variables.

4. Find the maximum possible value of the expression found in step 2.

5. Check whether the equation-condition holds true.

12. For positive real x, y and z, if $x + y + z = 12$, determine the minimum possible value of $x^2 + y^2 + z^2$.

Walk-Through

1. Cauchy-Schwarz inequality states that $(a^2 + b^2)(c^2 + d^2) \geq (ac + bd)^2$, and the equation holds true if $\dfrac{a}{c} = \dfrac{b}{d} = k$ for some k.

2. Likewise, $(a^2 + b^2 + c^2)(d^2 + e^2 + f^2) \geq (ad + be + cf)^2$. The equation holds true for $\dfrac{a}{d} = \dfrac{b}{e} = \dfrac{c}{f} = k$ for some k.

3. Apply step 2 to the given problem and find the minimum possible value of $x^2 + y^2 + z^2$.

13. For integer values of x, y, and z, if $x + y + z = 10$, and $x^2 + y^2 + z^2 = 204$, determine the maximum possible value of z.

Walk-Through

1. Set $x + y = 10 - z$.

2. Set $x^2 + y^2 = 204 - z^2$.

3. Apply Cauchy-Schwarz inequality to the left-side of the equations.

4. On the other hand, try $z^2 = 196$, and see if there are values of x and y holding the equation true, for the sake of using problem-solving strategies.

14. Let a, b, and c be real numbers such that $a + b + c = 1$. If $a \geq -\frac{2}{3}$, $b \geq -1$ and $c \geq -\frac{1}{3}$, the maximum possible value of

$$\sqrt{3a + 2} + \sqrt{3b + 3} + \sqrt{3c + 1}$$

can be written as $\sqrt{n}$ where n is a positive integer. Determine the exact value of n.

Walk-Through

1. Let $\sqrt{3a + 2} = x$, $\sqrt{3b + 3} = y$, and $\sqrt{3c + 1} = z$.

2. Apply QM-AM inequality. In particular, for valid r, s, and t,

$$\sqrt{\frac{r^2 + s^2 + t^2}{3}} \geq \frac{r + s + t}{3}.$$

15. If a polynomial $p(x) = x^3 - 12x^2 + cx + d$ has positive real roots r, s, and t, let $q(x) = (x + \sqrt{r})(x + \sqrt{s})(x + \sqrt{t})$ be a polynomial with real coefficients. If the coefficient of x^2 is k, determine the maximum possible value of k.

Walk-Through

1. Viete's formula implies that $r + s + t = 12$.

2. The coefficient of x^2 equals $\sqrt{r} + \sqrt{s} + \sqrt{t}$.

3. Apply QM-AM inequality for r, s, and t.

4. Find the maximum possible value of k by setting the inequality into equation.

16. Let $a_1, a_2, \cdots, a_n$ be non-negative real numbers such that $a_1 + a_2 + a_3 + \cdots + a_n = 1$. Given the following inequality

$$a_1^2 + a_2^2 + \cdots + a_n^2 \leq \frac{1}{1234},$$

determine the smallest possible natural value of n.

Walk-Through

1. One may apply Cauchy-Schwarz inequality with n-variables. In particular,

$$(a_1^2 + a_2^2 + \cdots + a_n^2)(1^2 + 1^2 + \cdots + 1^2) \geq (a_1 + a_2 + \cdots + a_n)^2$$

2. Also, one may apply QM-AM inequality. In particular,

$$\sqrt{\frac{a_1^2 + a_2^2 + \cdots + a_n^2}{n}} \geq \frac{a_1 + a_2 + a_3 + \cdots + a_n}{n}$$

3. Either by step 1 or 2, the smallest possible value of n occurs as a four-digit number. Retrieve the value and conclude solving the problem.

17. Given positive real r, s, and t, determine the smallest possible value of $\dfrac{\sqrt{r+s+t}}{\sqrt{r}+\sqrt{s}+\sqrt{t}}$.

> **Walk-Through**
>
> 1. Apply QM-AM inequality for r, s, and t.
>
> 2. Or, one may assume that the smallest possible value will be reached if $r = s = t = k$. Try substituting all letters as k and compare the given value with results found in step 1.

TOPIC 3 Ending with Combinatorics 271

18. Determine the value of k such that

$$3 + \frac{3+k}{4} + \frac{3+2k}{4^2} + \frac{3+3k}{4^3} \cdots = 8.$$

> **Walk-Through**
>
> 1. Find the sum of $3 + \frac{3}{4} + \frac{3}{4^2} + \cdots$.
>
> 2. Find the sum of $\frac{k}{4} + \frac{k}{4^2} + \frac{k}{4^3} + \cdots$.
>
> 3. Find the sum of $\frac{k}{4^2} + \frac{k}{4^3} + \frac{k}{4^4} + \cdots$.
>
> 4. Continuing this process infinitely many times to form another infinite geometric series.
>
> 5. Compute the sum and conclude solving the problem.

19. The following summation of binomial coefficients

$$\sum_{k=3}^{100} \frac{1}{\binom{k}{2}} = \frac{1}{\binom{3}{2}} + \frac{1}{\binom{4}{2}} + \frac{1}{\binom{5}{2}} + \cdots + \frac{1}{\binom{100}{2}}$$

can be written as $\dfrac{m}{n}$ where m and n are relatively prime positive integers. Determine $m + n$.

Walk-Through

1. Notice that $\dfrac{1}{\binom{k}{2}} = \dfrac{2}{k(k-1)} = 2\left(\dfrac{1}{k-1} - \dfrac{1}{k}\right)$.

2. This is known as telescoping series, so rewrite all of the sum in difference forms so that most of the terms are canceled.

3. Combine the remaining terms and conclude solving the problem.

20. Determine the largest prime divisor of

$$1^4 + 2^4 + 3^4 + \cdots + 15^4 + 16^4 + 17^4$$

> **Walk-Through**
>
> 1. This asks for finding one-to-one correspondence.
>
> 2. The summation equals the number of 5-tuples (a, b, c, d, e) such that $a < e$, $b < e$, $c < e$, and $d < e$, where all numbers range from 1 to 18.
>
> 3. Find the number of tuples of form (a, a, a, a, e).
>
> 4. Find the number of tuples of form (a, a, a, b, e).
>
> 5. Find the number of tuples of form (a, a, b, b, e).
>
> 6. Find the number of tuples of form (a, b, b, b, e).
>
> 7. Find the number of tuples of form (a, a, b, c, e).
>
> 8. Find the number of tuples of form (a, b, b, c, e).
>
> 9. Find the number of tuples of form (a, b, c, c, e).
>
> 10. Find the number of tuples of form (a, b, c, d, e).
>
> 11. Add all up and prime factorize to find the largest prime divisor.

21. Given an isosceles triangle ABC where $AB = BC$, the base angle is twice the vertex angle. The ratio $\dfrac{AB}{AC} = \dfrac{\sqrt{a}+b}{c}$ where a, b and c are square-free integers. Determine $a+b+c$.

> **Walk-Through**
>
> 1. This is a problem related to golden ratio. Let $AC = x$ and $AB = x+1$.
>
> 2. Using the angle bisector theorem, set up the ratio $x : x+1 = 1 : x$.
>
> 3. Solve for x, and find the exact value of $\dfrac{AB}{AC}$.

22. Given a parallelogram $ABCD$ such that $AB = 6$, $BC = 4$, if $m\angle ADC = 105°$, the area of parallelogram can be written as $a(\sqrt{b} + \sqrt{c})$ where a, b, and c are positive integers, and b and c are distinct square-free integers. Compute the sum of a, b, and c.

> **Walk-Through**
>
> 1. Use $\sin(A + B) = \sin(A)\cos(B) + \cos(A)\sin(B)$. The area of parallelogram is $ab\sin(\theta)$ where a and b are side lengths and θ is the angle formed between two adjacent sides.
>
> 2. Or, cut $75°$ into $15°$ and $60°$ to chase lengths for a triangle $15° - 75° - 90°$. Let the shorter side length be x, then notice that the longer side must be $2x + \sqrt{3}x$. Reason why it works this way.

23. Given a triangle ABC such that $AB = 10$, $BC = 9$, and $m\angle B = 48°$, let P be a point on $\overline{AC}$ such that $m\angle ABP = 30°$ and $m\angle CBP = 18°$. Then,

$$\frac{AP}{CP} = \frac{a\sqrt{a} + a}{b}$$

where a is a square-free integer and b is a positive integer. Determine ab.

Walk-Through

1. It is known that $\sin(2\theta) = 2\sin(\theta)\cos(\theta)$.

2. Likewise, it is known that
$$\cos(2\theta) = \cos^2(\theta) - \sin^2(\theta)$$
$$= 2\cos^2(\theta) - 1$$
$$= 1 - 2\sin^2(\theta)$$

3. According to the extended law of sines, $\dfrac{AP}{CP} = \dfrac{AB\sin(30°)}{BC\sin(18°)}$.

4. Find $\sin(18°)$ using step 2.

24. Given a triangle ABC where $AB = 6$, $BC = 7$, and $AC = 11$, there exists a point X on $\overline{AC}$ such that $AX - CX = 1$. The ratio

$$\frac{\sin(\angle ABX)}{\sin(\angle CBX)}$$

can be written as $\dfrac{m}{n}$ where m and n are relatively prime positive integers. Determine $m + n$.

Walk-Through

1. Find AX and CX.

2. According to the extended law of sines,

$$\frac{AX}{XC} = \frac{AB\sin(\angle ABX)}{BC\sin(\angle CBX)}$$

3. Use step 2 to find out the ratio as $\dfrac{m}{n}$.

25. In triangle ABC, where $AB = 5$, $BC = 7$, there is a cevian BD such that $2\angle ABD = \angle CBD$, where $m\angle ABC = \theta$. If $AD = 3$ and $CD = 6$, the value of $\cos(\theta)$ can be written as $\dfrac{m}{n}$ where m and n are relatively prime positive integers. Determine $m + n$.

Walk-Through

1. Reason why $\sin(2\theta) = 2\sin(\theta)\cos(\theta)$ from $\sin(A + B) = \sin(A)\cos(B) + \cos(A)\sin(B)$.

2. Use the extended law of sines to deduce the value of $\cos(\theta)$. In particular,
$$\frac{AD}{DC} = \frac{AB\sin(\theta)}{BC\sin(2\theta)}$$

26. In triangle ABC, $AB = AC$ and $\cos \angle A = \dfrac{1}{4}$. If points P and Q trisect $\overline{BC}$, find the value of $\tan^2 \angle PAQ$.

> **Walk-Through**
>
> 1. According to the law of cosines, $a^2 = b^2 + c^2 - 2bc \cos(A)$.
>
> 2. Let $BP = PQ = QC = k$.
>
> 3. Let $AB = x$.
>
> 4. Use the law of cosines to express x in terms of k.
>
> 5. Drop the altitude from A to $\overline{BC}$. Call the perpendicular foot as R.
>
> 6. Let θ be the angle measure of PAR.
>
> 7. Use the law of tangents - $\tan(A + B) = \dfrac{\tan(A) + \tan(B)}{1 - \tan(A)\tan(B)}$.
>
> 8. Notice that $\tan(\angle PAQ) = \tan(2\theta)$.

27. Given a scalene triangle ABC such that $A = 144°$, $AB = 4$, $AC = 5$, the exact value of BC^2 can be written as $a + b\sqrt{c}$ where a, b, and c are positive integers, and c is a square-free integer. Determine $a + b + c$.

Walk-Through

1. It is known that $\sin(\theta) = \sin(180° - \theta)$.

2. Also, it is known that $\cos(\theta) = -\cos(180° - \theta)$.

3. Use $\cos(36°) = \dfrac{1 + \sqrt{5}}{4}$.

4. Use the law of cosines to find out BC^2.

28. Given an acute isosceles triangle ABC where $AB = BC$, there exists some D in $\overline{BC}$. Let P and Q be the perpendicular feet from D to AB and to AC, respectively. If $DP = 25$, $BD = 65$, and $DQ = 52$, then AB can be written as $a + \dfrac{b}{c}\sqrt{d}$ where a, b, c, and d are positive integers such that d is a square-free integer. Determine $a + b + c + d$.

> **Walk-Through**
>
> 1. Use the angle bisector theorem on PD to find out a trigonometric ratio.
>
> 2. Use similar figures to find the length CD.
>
> 3. Notice that $AB = BD + CD$.
>
> 4. Find the exact value of a, b, c, and d, from $BD + CD$.

29. Given a triangle ABC where $AB = 13$, $BC = 15$, and $AC = 14$, there exists a point P on the incircle such that the distance from P to AC is 2, where P is closer to A than to C. The value of $\tan(\angle PAC)$ can be written as $\dfrac{a + \sqrt{a}}{b}$, where a and b are positive integers, and a is a square-free integer. Determine $a + b$.

Walk-Through

1. Draw an incircle with inradius. Label the incenter as I.

2. Draw the parallel line through P to $\overline{AC}$.

3. Label the perpendicular foot from P to $\overline{AC}$ as Q.

4. Let $AQ = k$. Set up Pythagorean Theorem with respect to k to find its value.

5. Set $\tan(\angle PAC) = \dfrac{2}{k}$ and simplify.

30. In the complex plane, let S be the set of all complex numbers of the form $3z + 2w$ where $|z| = 1$ and $|w| = 1$. Find the area of the region inside S.

> **Walk-Through**
>
> 1. Use $||z| - |w|| \leq |z + w| \leq |z| + |w|$, a triangular inequality of complex numbers.
>
> 2. Draw two circles centered at the origin on the complex plane.
>
> 3. Find the area of the region expressed in the inequality found in step 1.

31. Let $z = a + bi$ where a and b are positive real numbers. If $z^3 + 3|z|^2 - 5z = 0$, determine the exact value of $|z|^2$.

> **Walk-Through**
>
> 1. Use $|z|^2 = z\bar{z}$, where $|z| = \sqrt{a^2 + b^2}$ and $\bar{z}$ is the complex conjugate of z.
>
> 2. Let $z = a + bi$.
>
> 3. Take out z from the given equation.
>
> 4. Substitute $z = a + bi$ and $\bar{z} = a - bi$.
>
> 5. Find the exact value of a^2 and b^2.

32. Determine the exact value of

$$\cos\left(\frac{2\pi}{7}\right) + \cos\left(\frac{4\pi}{7}\right) + \cos\left(\frac{6\pi}{7}\right) + \cos\left(\frac{8\pi}{7}\right) + \cos\left(\frac{10\pi}{7}\right) + \cos\left(\frac{12\pi}{7}\right)$$

Walk-Through

1. It is known that

$$\cos(A) + \cos(B) = 2\cos\left(\frac{A+B}{2}\right)\cos\left(\frac{A-B}{2}\right)$$

$$\cos(A) - \cos(B) = -2\sin\left(\frac{A+B}{2}\right)\sin\left(\frac{A-B}{2}\right)$$

2. Also, notice that

$$\sin(3\theta) = 3\sin(\theta) - 4\sin^3(\theta)$$

$$\cos(3\theta) = 4\cos^3(\theta) - 3\cos(\theta)$$

3. Use step 1 and 2 to simplify the given expression.

33. Let z be a complex number such that $\left|z + \dfrac{1}{z}\right| = 2$. Find the largest possible value of $|z|$.

Walk-Through

1. Square the given expression.

2. Use $|z|^2 = z\bar{z}$.

3. Let $z = r(\theta) = re^{i\theta}$. This implies that $\bar{z} = r(-\theta) = re^{-i\theta}$.

4. Simplify $\dfrac{z}{\bar{z}} + \dfrac{\bar{z}}{z}$, using step 2.

5. Set up an equality for $|z|^2 + \dfrac{1}{|z|^2}$.

6. Solve for the largest possible value of $|z|$.

34. Let ABC be a right triangle with hypotenuse AC. Let G be the centroid of this triangle and suppose that we have $AG^2 + BG^2 + CG^2 = 48$. Find AC^2.

> **Walk-Through**
>
> 1. Label half of AB as a.
>
> 2. Label half of BC as b.
>
> 3. Likewise, label half of AC as c.
>
> 4. Set up three Pythagorean equations to find AG^2, BG^2 and CG^2.
>
> 5. Compute AC^2.

35. Given a parallelogram $ABCD$ where $A = (10, 10)$, $B = (15, 11)$, $C = (17, 14)$, and $D = (12, 13)$, then the area of parallelogram can be written as a natural value of n. Determine the exact value of n.

Walk-Through

1. Move all $ABCD$ to $A'B'C'D'$ by translation $<x', y'> = <x-10, y-10>$.

2. Notice that translation preserves congruence, so the area of $ABCD$ equals that of $A'B'C'D'$.

3. Apply the shoelace theorem on $A'B'C'D'$ to find out the area of $ABCD$.

Answer Key

1. 17

For $x^2 - nx + 2n = 0$ to have rational roots, the discriminant must be a perfect square. Hence, $n^2 - 8n = k^2$ for some integer k. Hence, $n^2 - 8n + 16 = k^2 + 16$ implies that $(n-4)^2 - k^2 = 16$. Thus, $(n-4-k)(n-4+k) = 16$ illustrates that $2(n-4) = 10$ or 8. Hence, $n - 4 = 5$ or 4. Therefore, $n = 9$ or 8. The sum of these values equals 17.

2. 11

Notice that
$x^4 - x^2 - 1 = (x-r_1)(x-r_2)(x-r_3)(x-r_4)$.
Then, substitute $x = -2$ into the equation to find out
$(-2)^4 - (-2)^2 - 1 = (-2-r_1)(-2-r_2)(-2-r_3)(-2-r_4) = (2+r_1)(2+r_2)(2+r_3)(2+r_4)$.
Hence, the answer equals 11.

3. 13

Consider a polynomial $(x-r)(x-s)(x-t)$. Then, according to the given condition, we set $x^3 - 3x^2 + 3x - 10 = 0$. Basic algebraic manipulation shows that $x^3 - 3x^2 + 3x - 1 = 10 - 1 = 9$. Hence, $(x-1)^3 = 9$. Therefore, the real r must be $\sqrt[3]{9} + 1$. The sum of a, b, and c is $3 + 9 + 1 = 13$.

4. 6

Solution 1.
Let $p(x) = x^3 - 5x^2 + 6x - 1$. Then, $p\left(\dfrac{1}{x}\right) = 0$ has roots $x = \dfrac{1}{r}, \dfrac{1}{s}$, and $\dfrac{1}{t}$.
Since $p\left(\dfrac{1}{x}\right)$ is not polynomial, we let $q(x) = x^3 p\left(\dfrac{1}{x}\right)$, which has the same reciprocal roots. Notice that $q(x) = -x^3 + 6x^2 - 5x + 1$. Since $\dfrac{1}{r} + \dfrac{1}{s} + \dfrac{1}{t}$ is the sum of roots, we get 6.

Solution 2.
According to Viete's formula, we get $r + s + t = 5$, $rs + st + tr = 6$ and $rst = 1$.
Since $\dfrac{1}{r} + \dfrac{1}{s} + \dfrac{1}{t} = \dfrac{rs + st + tr}{rst}$, we get the answer 6.

5. 277

According to Newton's identity, we get
$S_1 = 5$, $S_2 - 5S_1 + 4(2) = 0$,
$S_3 - 5S_2 + 4S_1 - 1(3) = 0$, and
$S_4 - 5S_3 + 4S_2 - S_1 = 0$. Thus, $S_1 = 5$, $S_2 = 17$, $S_3 = 68$. Since
$S_4 = 5S_3 - 4S_2 + S_1$, we get $S_4 = 277$.

6. 6

Notice that $r + s + t = 5$. Then, according to the given condition, $p(x) = 5 - x$ for $x = r, s$, and t, i.e.,
$p(x) - 5 + x = (x-r)(x-s)(x-t)$, for $p(x)$ is a cubic polynomial.

Therefore,

$$p(1) - 5 + 1$$
$$= (1-r)(1-s)(1-t)$$
$$= 1 - 5 + 7 - 1$$
$$= 2.$$

Therefore, $p(1) - 4 = 2$, so $p(1) = 6$.

7. 4

Consider a polynomial
$(x-r)(x-s) = x^2 - (r+s)x + rs = x^2 - kx + k$.
There exist real r and s such that $x^2 - kx + k = 0$ at $x = r$ and $x = s$. This implies that the discriminant is at least 0. Thus, $k^2 - 4k \geq 0$ implies that $k \geq 4$ for positive real k. The smallest possible value of k is 4.

8. 1002

$$\frac{(a+b)(b+c)(a+c)}{abc}$$
$$= \frac{a^2b + ab^2 + ca^2 + 2abc + b^2c + c^2a + bc^2}{abc}$$
$$= \frac{ab(a+b) + ca(a+c) + bc(b+c) + 2abc}{abc}$$
$$= \frac{a+b}{c} + \frac{b+c}{a} + \frac{a+c}{b} + 2$$
$$= 1000 + 2$$
$$= 1002$$

9. 4

$$a^4 + 4b^2$$
$$= a^4 + 4a^2b^2 + 4b^2 - 4a^2b^2$$
$$= (a^2 + 2b^2)^2 - (2ab)^2$$
$$= (a^2 - 2ab + 2b^2)(a^2 + 2ab + 2b^2)$$
$$= (2)(520)$$
$$= (4)(260)$$
$$= \vdots$$

Out of all pairs, $(a^2 - 2ab + 2b^2)(a^2 + 2ab + 2b^2) = (20)(52)$ is the only possible solution. Hence, $a^2 = 4$ and $b^2 = 16$. Thus, $(a, b) = (\pm 2, \pm 4)$ and $(\pm 2, \mp 4)$. Therefore, there are 4 pairs.

10. 17

Expand $(x-y)^2 + (y-z)^2 + (z-x)^2 = 41$ into $2(x^2 + y^2 + z^2) - 2(xy + yz + zx) = 41$. Then, $2(xy + yz + zx) = 179$. Hence,

$$(x+y+z)^2$$
$$= x^2 + y^2 + z^2 + 2(xy + yz + zx)$$
$$= 110 + 179$$
$$= 289.$$

Thus, $x + y + z = \sqrt{289} = 17$.

11. 64

In order to have maximum possible volume of parallelepiped, we set x, y, and z positive real. Then, according to AM-GM inequality,

$$\frac{x+y+z}{3} \geq \sqrt[3]{xyz}$$

Hence, $xyz \leq 64$. Since the volume of the parallelepiped is determined by the product of x, y and z, we get the maximum possible value as 64.

12. 48

According to Cauchy-Schwarz inequality, we get

$$(x+y+z)^2 \leq (x^2+y^2+z^2)(1^2+1^2+1^2).$$

Hence, $x^2+y^2+z^2 \geq \dfrac{144}{3} = 48$. The equality holds true if $x = y = z = 4$.

13. 14

Solution 1. According to Cauchy-Schwarz inequality, $(x+y)^2 \leq (x^2+y^2)(1^2+1^2)$. In other words, $(10-z)^2 \leq (204-z^2)(2)$. This implies that $3z^2 - 20z - 308 \leq 0$, i.e., $(3z+22)(z-14) \leq 0$. Thus, the largest possible positive real value of z must be 14.

Solution 2. Since x, y, and z are integers, we use that $z^2 \leq 204$. Since $z \leq 14$, we plug $z = 14$ to check that $x = y = -2$ satisfy the given equation. Hence, $z = 14$ is the largest possible value of z.

14. 27

According to QM-AM inequality,

$$\sqrt{\dfrac{3a+2+3b+3+3c+1}{3}} \geq$$
$$\dfrac{\sqrt{3a+2}+\sqrt{3b+3}+\sqrt{3c+1}}{3}$$
$$\sqrt{\dfrac{3(a+b+c)+6}{3}} \geq$$
$$\dfrac{\sqrt{3a+2}+\sqrt{3b+3}+\sqrt{3c+1}}{3}$$
$$\sqrt{3} \geq \dfrac{\sqrt{3a+2}+\sqrt{3b+3}+\sqrt{3c+1}}{3}$$
$$3\sqrt{3} \geq \sqrt{3a+2}+\sqrt{3b+3}+\sqrt{3c+1}$$
$$\sqrt{27} \geq \sqrt{3a+2}+\sqrt{3b+3}+\sqrt{3c+1}$$

15. 6

According to Viete's formula, we know that $r+s+t = 12$. Now, according to QM-AM inequality, we set

$$\sqrt{\dfrac{r+s+t}{3}} \geq \dfrac{\sqrt{r}+\sqrt{s}+\sqrt{t}}{3}$$

Hence, $\sqrt{r}+\sqrt{s}+\sqrt{t} \leq 3\sqrt{4} = 6$. Since $k = \sqrt{r}+\sqrt{s}+\sqrt{t}$, we conclude that the maximum possible value of k is 6.

16. 1234

According to QM-AM inequality, we notice that

$$\sqrt{\dfrac{1}{1234n}} \geq \sqrt{\dfrac{a_1^2+a_2^2+\cdots+a_n^2}{n}} \geq \dfrac{1}{n}$$

since $a_1+a_2+\cdots+a_n = 1$. Hence, we conclude that $\dfrac{1}{1234n} \geq \dfrac{1}{n^2}$. This implies that $n \geq 1234$. The smallest possible value must be 1234.

17. $\dfrac{\sqrt{3}}{3}$

Solution 1. According to QM-AM inequality, for positive real r, s, and t,
$$\sqrt{\dfrac{r+s+t}{3}} \geq \dfrac{\sqrt{r}+\sqrt{s}+\sqrt{t}}{3}$$
Thus, $\dfrac{\sqrt{r+s+t}}{\sqrt{r}+\sqrt{s}+\sqrt{t}} \geq \dfrac{\sqrt{3}}{3}$.

Solution 2. The smallest possible value will be reached if $r=s=t=k$ for some real k. Then, $\dfrac{\sqrt{r+s+t}}{\sqrt{r}+\sqrt{s}+\sqrt{t}} = \dfrac{\sqrt{3k}}{3\sqrt{k}} = \dfrac{\sqrt{3}}{3}$.

18. 9

Let $S = 3 + \dfrac{3+k}{4} + \dfrac{3+2k}{4^2} + \cdots$. Then, $\dfrac{S}{4} = \dfrac{3}{4} + \dfrac{3+k}{4^2} + \dfrac{3+2k}{4^3} + \cdots$. Subtracting S by $\dfrac{S}{4}$, we get $3 + \dfrac{k}{4} + \dfrac{k}{4^2} + \cdots$. Hence, $\dfrac{3}{4}S = 3 + \dfrac{k/4}{1-1/4}$, so $k=9$.

19. 99

The summation looks like a telescoping series, and the given expression turns into $2\left(\dfrac{1}{2} - \dfrac{1}{3} + \dfrac{1}{3} - \dfrac{1}{4} + \cdots + \dfrac{1}{99} - \dfrac{1}{100}\right)$. Hence, the given series equals $\dfrac{49}{50}$, so $m+n = 49+50 = 99$.

20. 131

In order to solve this problem, we must deduce a formula for the given summation. Let $(a_1, a_2, a_3, a_4, a_5)$ be a 5-tuple such that $1 \leq a_i \leq 18$.

Then, the given summation is exactly equal to finding the number of 5-tuples such that $a_1 < a_5$, $a_2 < a_5$, $a_3 < a_5$, and $a_4 < a_5$. If $a_5 = 2$, then the number of 5-tuples equals 1^4.

If $a_5 = 3$, then the number of 5-tuples equals 2^4. Keep continuing this process until we have $a_5 = 18$, so that there are 17^4 number of 5-tuples. Now, the next step is to figure out the types of 5-tuples. Here is the total number of 5-tuple types, where a, b, c, d, and e are different integers.

1. (a,a,a,a,b) : there are $\binom{18}{2} = 153$ tuples.

2. (a,a,a,b,c) : there are $\binom{18}{3}\dfrac{4!}{3!1!} = 3264$ tuples.

3. (a,a,b,b,c) : there are $\binom{18}{3}\dfrac{4!}{2!2!} = 4896$ tuples.

4. (a,b,b,b,c) : there are $\binom{18}{3}\dfrac{4!}{3!1!} = 3264$ tuples.

5. (a,a,b,c,d) : there are $\binom{18}{4}\dfrac{4!}{2!} = 36720$ tuples.

6. (a,b,b,c,d) : there are $\binom{18}{4}\dfrac{4!}{2!} = 36720$ tuples.

7. (a,b,c,c,d) : there are $\binom{18}{4}\dfrac{4!}{2!} = 36720$ tuples.

8. (a,b,c,d,e) : there are $\binom{18}{5}4! = 205632$ tuples.

Hence, the total number of 5-tuples equals 327369.

Since the prime factorization of 327369 can be written as $3 \times 7^2 \times 17 \times 131$, we conclude that the largest prime factor that divides the given summation is 131.

21. 8

Let α be the vertex angle. Then, $5\alpha = 180°$ implies that $\alpha = 36°$. Let $AB = BC = x$ and $AC = y$. Then, $\dfrac{x}{y} = \dfrac{\sin(2\alpha)}{\sin(\alpha)} = 2\cos(\alpha) = 2\dfrac{1+\sqrt{5}}{4} = \dfrac{1+\sqrt{5}}{2}$.
Hence, $a + b + c = 1 + 5 + 2 = 8$.

22. 14

The area of the parallelogram can be found by $4 \times 6 \times \sin(105°)$, where $\sin(105°) = \sin(60°)\cos(45°) + \cos(45°)\sin(60°) = \dfrac{\sqrt{6}+\sqrt{2}}{4}$. Hence, the area can be written as $6(\sqrt{6}+\sqrt{2})$, so $6 + 6 + 2 = 14$.

23. 45

According to the extended law of sines, $\dfrac{AP}{CP} = \dfrac{AB\sin(30°)}{BC\sin(18°)} = \dfrac{10\sin(30°)}{9\sin(18°)} = \dfrac{10}{9} \times \dfrac{1/2}{(\sqrt{5}-1)/4} = \dfrac{5\sqrt{5}+5}{9}$. Hence, $ab = 5(9) = 45$.

24. 12

According to the extended law of sines, $\dfrac{6}{5} = \dfrac{6\sin(\angle ABX)}{7\sin(\angle CBX)}$. Hence, $\dfrac{\sin(\angle ABX)}{\sin(\angle CBX)} = \dfrac{6}{5} \times \dfrac{7}{6} = \dfrac{7}{5}$. Hence, $m + n = 7 + 5 = 12$.

25. 12

Let $m\angle ABD = \theta$. According to the extended law of sines, $\dfrac{5\sin(\theta)}{7\sin(2\theta)} = \dfrac{3}{6}$. Hence, $\dfrac{5\sin\theta}{7\sin 2\theta} = \dfrac{5\sin\theta}{14\sin\theta\cos\theta} = \dfrac{3}{6}$, so $\cos\theta = \dfrac{5}{7}$. Hence, $m + n = 12$.

26. $\dfrac{15}{49}$

Assume that the midpoint of $\overline{BC}$ is D. Let $m\angle B = m\angle C = \phi$. Then, $2\phi + A = 180°$, so $\cos(2\phi) = \cos(180° - A) = -\cos(A) = -\dfrac{1}{4}$. Hence, $2\cos^2(\phi) - 1 = -\dfrac{1}{4}$. This implies that $\cos(\phi) = \dfrac{\sqrt{3}}{\sqrt{8}}$. Thus, let $AB = AC = \sqrt{8}k$ and $BD = CD = \sqrt{3}k$.

Since $BP = PQ = QC$ and $3BP = 2\sqrt{3}k$, we conclude that $PD = DQ = \dfrac{\sqrt{3}}{3}k$. Let $m\angle PAD = m\angle QAD = \alpha$. Then, $\tan(\alpha) = \dfrac{1}{\sqrt{15}}$. Since $\tan(2\alpha) = \dfrac{2/\sqrt{15}}{1 - 1/15} = \dfrac{\sqrt{15}}{7}$. Thus, $\tan^2(\angle PAQ) = \dfrac{15}{49}$.

27. 66

$BC^2 = 4^2 + 5^2 - 2(4)(5)\cos(144°)$. Notice that $\cos(144°) = -\cos(36°)$, so $BC^2 = 51 + 10\sqrt{5}$, so $a + b + c = 51 + 10 + 5 = 66$.

28. 148

Let $m\angle DBP = \theta$. Then, $\tan(\theta) = \dfrac{5}{12}$. Let $\tan\left(\dfrac{\theta}{2}\right) = t$. Then, $\dfrac{5}{12} = \dfrac{2t}{1-t^2}$. Hence, $t = \dfrac{1}{5}$. Since $DQ = 52$, we conclude that $CD = \dfrac{52}{5}\sqrt{26}$ by Pythagorean Theorem. Hence, $BC = 65 + \dfrac{52}{5}\sqrt{26}$. Thus, $a+b+c+d = 65+52+5+26 = 148$.

29. 9

Let $m\angle PAC = \theta$. Also, let the perpendicular foot from P to $\overline{BC}$ be Q. Then, let $AQ = k$. Also, let the point of tangency between the incircle and $\overline{BC}$ be R. Then, $QR = 6-k$ by length chasing. Since the inradius is 4, we get a right triangle formed by the horizontal line passing through P, the vertical line passing through R and $\overline{PI}$ where I is the incenter. Its side lengths are given by 4, 2, and $6-k$ by length chasing. Hence, $6-k = 2\sqrt{3}$, so $k = 6-2\sqrt{3}$. Since $\tan(\theta) = \dfrac{2}{k}$, we conclude that $\tan(\theta) = \dfrac{1}{3-\sqrt{3}} = \dfrac{3+\sqrt{3}}{6}$. Thus, $a+b = 3+6 = 9$.

30. 24π

Let $x = 3z + 2\omega$ where $|z|=1$ and $|\omega|=1$. Then, by triangular inequality, $|x| = |3z+2\omega| \le |3z|+|2\omega| = 5$ and $|x| = |3z+2\omega| \ge |3z|-|2\omega| = 1$. Hence, the area of all x in the complex plane is 24π.

31. 4

$z^3 + 3|z|^2 - 5z = 0$. Notice that $z^3 + 3z\bar{z} - 5z = 0$. Since $z \ne 0$, we get $z^2 + 3\bar{z} - 5 = 0$. Let $z = a+bi$. Then, $(a+bi)^2 + 3(a-bi) - 5 = 0$. Thus, $a^2 + 2abi - b^2 + 3a - 3bi - 5 = 0$. Hence, $(a^2 - b^2 + 3a - 5) + (2ab - 3b)i = 0$. Therefore, $2ab - 3b$ implies that $2a = 3$. Plug $a = \dfrac{3}{2}$ into $a^2 - b^2 + 3a - 5 =$. Thus, $\dfrac{9}{4} - b^2 + \dfrac{9}{2} - 5 = 0$. This implies that $b^2 = \dfrac{7}{4}$. Since $|z|^2 = a^2 + b^2 = \dfrac{9}{4} + \dfrac{7}{4} = 4$.

32. -1

Notice that $\cos\dfrac{2\pi}{7} + \cos\dfrac{12\pi}{7} = 2\cos\pi\cos\dfrac{5\pi}{7}$. Likewise, notice that $\cos\dfrac{4\pi}{7} + \cos\dfrac{10\pi}{7} = 2\cos\pi\cos\dfrac{3\pi}{7}$. Lastly, notice that $\cos\dfrac{6\pi}{7} + \cos\dfrac{8\pi}{7} = 2\cos\pi\cos\dfrac{\pi}{7}$. Hence, $2\cos\pi(\cos\dfrac{\pi}{7} + \cos\dfrac{3\pi}{7} + \cos\dfrac{5\pi}{7}) = -2\left(\dfrac{1}{2}\right) = -1$.

Let's see why $\cos\dfrac{\pi}{7} + \cos\dfrac{3\pi}{7} + \cos\dfrac{5\pi}{7} = \dfrac{1}{2}$. Notice that $\cos\dfrac{3\pi}{7} + \cos\dfrac{5\pi}{7} = 2\cos\dfrac{\pi}{7}\cos\dfrac{4\pi}{7}$. Since $\cos\dfrac{\pi}{7} = \dfrac{\sin(2\pi/7)}{2\sin(\pi/7)}$ and $\cos\dfrac{4\pi}{7} = 1 - 2\sin^2\dfrac{2\pi}{7}$, we can write the original expression as

$$\dfrac{3\sin(2\pi/7) - 4\sin^3(2\pi/7)}{2\sin(\pi/7)} = \dfrac{\sin(6\pi/7)}{2\sin(\pi/7)} = \dfrac{1}{2}.$$

33. $\sqrt{2}+1$

If $|z+\frac{1}{z}|=2$, then
$(z+\frac{1}{z})(\bar{z}+\frac{1}{\bar{z}})=|z|^2+2\cos(2\theta)+\frac{1}{|z|^2}=4.$
Since $4-2\cos(2\theta)\leq 6$, we conclude that
$|z|^2+\frac{1}{|z|^2}\leq 6.$ Let $k=|z|^2\geq 0.$ Then,
$k+\frac{1}{k}\leq 6$ implies that $k^2-6k+1\leq 0.$
Thus, $|z|^2=k\leq 3+2\sqrt{2}.$ The largest possible value of $|z|$ equals $\sqrt{2}+1.$

34. 72

Let half of AB be a, half of BC be b and half of AC be c. Then, $AG^2=\frac{4}{9}(4a^2+b^2)$, $CG^2=\frac{4}{9}(a^2+4b^2)$ and $BG^2=\frac{4}{9}(a^2+b^2).$
Thus, $\frac{24}{9}(a^2+b^2)=48$ indicates that $a^2+b^2=18.$ Hence, $4a^2+4b^2=AC^2=72.$

35. 13

Solution 1. Using a shoelace theorem, we get the area of parallelogram as 13, i.e.
$\frac{1}{2}(10(11)+15(14)+17(13)+12(10))-(10(15)+11(17)+14(12)+13(10))=13.$

Solution 2. Using a matrix determinant, we get the area of parallelogram as 13.
Let $\vec{u}=<15,11>-<10,10>=<5,1>$
and $\vec{v}=<12,13>-<10,10>=<2,3>.$
Hence, its determinant equals
$|5(3)-1(2)|=13.$